144,000 HARPS

The Hidden Songs of Israel

A  Book ©

Hollisa Alewine

CONTENTS

Gabriel Bello, composer, producer, and performer of Billboard jazz and gospel hits, writes of *144,000 Harps*:

As a professional musician of 25+ years and minister of 20+ years, this book by Sister Hollisa has caused me to deeply reflect upon how much I've missed in my studies and how I perform both of these duties. The insight into the ordained songs and incredible depth of wisdom and knowledge therein should give any believer, follower of Messiah/Christ, cause to study, reflect, then act. For those who are also musicians, especially leaders of music, worship, and praise in His Church, this should be required reading.

The relationship between these songs, prophecy, Kingdom order, history, the Hebrew language, scientific properties, musical intervals and how Adonai ordains songs should give any one, but especially musicians/minstrels, hours of material to investigate. Each chapter took me hours to chew through as I wanted to fully grasp the information, knowledge, and transform it into practice, applicable wisdom as a working musician and minister.

She also threw in some of her trademark dry wit humor, if you're paying attention. The Hebrew, the traditions, the historical references, the musical revelations of the Hebrew cantillations and shalshelet were astounding. I mean mind blowing! The significance of music and the 10 biblical songs are amplified to "11" in this work. Personally, I will be re-reading 144,000 Harps for months, if not years to come, for deep cries out to deep. I am indebted to Sister Alewine for sharing her studies and discoveries.

https://www.gabrielbellomusic.com

GLOSSARY

Adonai – my Lord.

HaBrit HaChadasha – New Testament. In Hebrew, literally, "Renewed Covenant." The Hebrew word for new, *chadash*, also means renewed, as we apply the adjective to the "new" moon each month. The moon is not new; it is the same moon. Its appearance from human perspective is merely renewed each month. By the same token, Jeremiah 31:31 defines the terms of the New Covenant: the Torah will be written on the hearts of God's people. It is not a new Torah, but the *only* Torah renewed in a dynamic way because of the work of Yeshua, a better mediator than Moses.

Cantillation (mark) – a melodic mode attached to individual signs that mark the Hebrew text of the Scriptures for chanting or singing in the synagogue. Although Mizrachi (Oriental), Sephardic (Spanish), and Ashkenazic (European) interpretations of the signs vary, similarities at important points indicate a common origin in Temple times.

Chok(im) – ordinances of the Torah which have no rational explanation; the only explanation is that "you are to be holy for I am holy."

Contranym – word that functions as its own opposite, like the English word "cleave," which means both to cut away as well as to cling tightly.

Elohim – God, the Creator.

Erev Shabbat – Literally "evening Shabbat" Friday evening at sunset.

Equivalence of expression – an equivalent expression

will explain a certain expression of the compared word or phrase. It is not exactly the same, but equivalent in essence. It may be a metaphorical definition or descriptor, such as "The Torah (law) is a **light**; the commandment is a **lamp**."

Haggadah – The Haggadah is a book that contains the order of the Passover service. It comes from a Hebrew word *haggid*, which means "telling." The Passover service in each home requires the telling of the events of the Exodus each year.

Haftorah – portion of Scripture from the Prophets that is read along with the customary portion of the Torah read in a particular week

Ha-Makom – literally, "The Place." Refers to Mount Moriah in Jerusalem, the location where Abraham offered Isaac as a sacrifice and the place where the First and Second Temple were built.

Hermeneutics – Methods of Biblical interpretation applying accepted rules of interpretation.

Ketuvim – the section of the TANAKH known as the Writings; it contains books such as the Psalms and the Book of Esther.

The Killir – was Eleazar ben Kalir, also known as Eleazar HaKalir or Eleazar ben Killir (AD 570 – AD 640) was a Near Eastern Jewish poet and songwriter. He wrote Hebrew poetry in classical liturgical verse, known as *piyut*. His songs continue to be sung into the modern era in religious services, such as Tisha B'Av, and particularly on the sabbath after a wedding. He wrote verses for all Jewish festivals, high Sabbaths, and fasts.

Menorah – a lampstand, specifically, the 7-branched golden lampstand that stood in the Holy Place of the Tabernacle and Temple.

Mikveh – a pool of living water for immersion, similar to the Christian baptistry

Mishnah – the Jewish oral law traditionally believed to have been passed down from Moses. Yeshua usually upheld the oral law of the House of Hillel, but he overruled most of the oral laws of the House of Shammai. They were the two predominant schools of the Pharisees in the First Century. Yeshua's method of determining the validity of oral law was to judge whether it set aside a written commandment in favor of the traditions of men.

Mishpat(im) – judgments. The mishpatim often deal with ethical or moral laws; they are logical and the rationale behind them is easy to understand.

Mitzvah – a commandment; there are Ten Words, known as the Ten Commandments, but the total of commandments as applied to various groups such as farmers, merchants, parents, children, priests, Levites, husbands, wives, neighbors, etc., in the Torah is 613.

Moed(im) – alludes to seasons and the appointed feasts of Israel: Passover, Unleavened Bread, Firstfruits of the Barley, Firstfruits of the Wheat (Pentecost), Trumpets, Day of Atonement, and Tabernacles

Nefesh – the bundle of appetites, desires, emotion, and intellect.

Rebbe/Rabbi – a Jewish spiritual leader or teacher.

Parasha – Each Shabbat is a public reading from the Scriptures: the *Torah* (Books of Moses/Law,) the *Haftorah* (Books of the Prophets) and the *Brit HaChadasha* (Renewed Covenant). Messianics read selected passages from the Torah and the Prophets every Sabbath as was done in Yeshua's day. This selected reading is called the *parasha*. Additionally, Messianics also read from the New

Testament (Renewed Covenant). Plural: *parshiot*.

Seder – order; it can refer to an order of service, such as a Passover seder.

Shabbat – the seventh day of the week in which work is proscribed.

Shema – the greatest commandment and the Jewish statement of faith:

> Hear, O Israel, the LORD is our God, the LORD is One. Blessed is the name of His glorious kingdom for all eternity. And you shall love the LORD your God with all your heart, with all your soul, and with all your might. And have these words, which I command you this day, be upon your heart. And you shall teach them diligently to your children, and speak of them when you sit in your house, when you walk by the way, when you retire, and when you arise. And you shall bind them for a sign upon your hand and let them be frontlets between your eyes. And you shall write them on the doorposts of your house and on your gates.

Shofar – ram's horn used as a trumpet for new moon (month) proclamations and feast days.

Seder – the order of the home Passover service and meal.

Sefer – book.

Siddur – a prayerbook.

Sofer – scribe.

Talmud – the largest body of Jewish law and commentary containing the Mishnah, Gemara, and Tosefta.

Tanakh – Old Testament. Tanakh is an acronym for Torah, Neviim, Ketuvim, or Law, Prophets, and Writings, the ancient divisions of the Hebrew Bible. The books of the Tanakh are the same as, but are not arranged in the same order as Christian Bibles.

Targum – an ancient Aramaic translation of the Hebrew Scriptures from around the 2nd Century A.D. Targum Yonatan and Targum Pseudo-Yonatan are the two most commonly-referenced to see how the Hebrew Scriptures were explained to those who spoke a different language. This gives the modern reader a grasp on how a specific passage or phrase was understood in the 1st-2nd Centuries.

Torah – the first five books of the Bible, misunderstood as "law" in English translations. The Torah is more accurately God's teaching and instruction. It contains topics such as science, history, priestly procedures, civil statutes, ordinances, health, agriculture, commandments, prophecies, prayer, animal husbandry, architecture, civics, and many others. The root word of Torah comes from the Hebrew word *yarah*, which means "to hit the mark." Torah may also be used to refer to all of the Hebrew Bible, or even to its smallest meaning, a procedure. Torah may be used by Messianic Jews to refer to the entire Bible from Genesis to Revelation, for the Torah is the foundation for all the Scriptures. The Prophets point Israel back to the Torah. The Psalms teach one to love the Torah as King David loved it. The Writings teach the consequences of departing from the Torah and the rewards for returning to it. The New Testament brings the Torah to its fullest meaning in the person Yeshua the Messiah, and much of the New Testament quotes the Tanakh.

Yeshua – Jesus' Hebrew name; salvation.

PREFACE

In synagogues around the world every Shabbat is a public reading from the Scriptures: the *Torah* (Books of Moses/Law,) and the *Haftorah* (Books of the Prophets). These are selected passages from the Torah and the Prophets for every Sabbath as was done in Yeshua's day. This selected reading is called the *parasha*. Additionally, Messianic Jews and non-Jews also read from the New Testament, the *Brit HaChadasha* (Renewed Covenant).

Reading the Scriptures on a set schedule is an ancient practice. Yeshua attended synagogue and read the selected Scripture aloud in Luke 4:16-17, "... as his custom was, he went into the synagogue on the Sabbath day, and *stood up for to read*. The scroll of the prophet Isaiah was handed to him." It was not by chance that this scroll was the Book of Isaiah. A portion of Isaiah was the scheduled reading for that Shabbat.

The public reading of Scripture dates back to Moses when he commanded the people to read them aloud at a religious gathering.[1] In Nehemiah 8, Ezra reemphasized the public reading as well as "... making it clear and giving the meaning so that the people could understand what was being read." Both Messianic Jews and Gentiles were expected to attend synagogue to "hear Moses," for Acts 15:21 documents the expectation that all would follow that tradition in order to hear the Scriptures, for only the wealthiest of families could afford a scroll of the Torah, Prophets, or Writings (including Psalms). What a blessing that modern families can read the Scriptures each day from their own Bibles!

In Acts 13:14-16, Paul, as was his custom with his companions, goes "...into the synagogue on the

1. Dt 31:11-12

13

Sabbath day, and sat down. And after the reading of the law and prophets..." Paul participates in the traditional Shabbat service, and he admonishes Timothy: "Until I come, devote yourself to the public reading of the Scripture, to preaching, and to teaching."[2] The Scripture referred to here is the Older Covenant (TANAKH). The Renewed Covenant (New Testament), as it is now, was not recognized by the Church until 367 A.D.

There are more reasons why believers benefit from reading the Torah and Prophets on Shabbat. In Acts 15, the apostles meet to discuss those born Gentiles leaving idolatry to follow Yeshua:

> It is my judgment, therefore, that we should not make it difficult for the Gentiles who are turning to God. Instead, we should write to them, telling them to abstain from food polluted by idols, from sexual immorality, from the meat of strangled animals, and from blood. For Moses has been preached in every city from the earliest times and *is read in the synagogues on every Sabbath.*

The implication is that non-Jews will learn more than the four "beginner" commandments and be taught how to be holy and pleasing to God as they attend synagogue every week and hear God's Word read aloud. Pursuing God's Word in the Torah is a blessing, not a yoke, and putting one foot forward at a time is healthy and right.

It is not surprising then, that much of the apostolic Scriptures and prophecies are founded upon the Torah. These books of "Moses" are different from the rest of the TANAKH. While the prophets received their messages in visions, dreams, and dark sayings, Moses received the Torah face to face:

2. I Ti 4:13

14

Hear now My words:
If there is a prophet among you, I, the
Lord, shall make Myself known to him
in a vision. I shall speak with him in a
dream. Not so, with My servant Moses,
he is faithful in all My household; with
him I speak mouth to mouth, even
openly, and not in dark sayings, and
he beholds the form of the Lord. (Nu
12:6-8)

Torah is the most direct of prophecies, yet it is often
dismissed as Bible stories. Indeed, the narratives
are splendid stories. Human beings learn first life
lessons through story tales, poems, songs, myths, and
storybooks. Likewise, the Torah is a believer's first
life lessons in faith. That's the beauty of the Word.
What appears to be stories holds the most powerful
of prophecies. It's not that the prophecies are
disguised, but when the reader is conditioned to see
only stories, then only stories will she see!

For this reason, reading the weekly *parasha* is
beneficial to the whole family. For children, it is
the essential history of faith through the stories. For
young people, it is inspiration and modeling of faith.
For adults, it is prophecy. For all, it decodes the
apocalyptic prophecies of the rest of the Bible.

Each parasha has a name.[3] That name is derived
from the first or from among the first words of the
parasha. The name provides a wonderful summary
of the key theme of the portion. For instance, the
first parasha is Bereishit (*B'ray-sheet*), which is the
contraction forming the first word of the Hebrew
Bible. Bereishit means, "In the beginning." In fact,
if strung together, the names of the Torah portions
provide a summary statement of an entire book of
the Torah. For an example, turn to Appendix B.

3. See Appendix
A for a list of
parshiot (plural)
names and their
meanings.

Look for a weekly parasha to be listed at the
beginning of some of this book's chapters. This

15

provides the reader with the complete contextual fabric from which the "song" is sung.

1

SONG AND DANCE: THE RESURRECTION STORY OF BETH-EL AND LUZ

Vayeitze "And went out"
Genesis 28:10-32:3
Hosea 12:13-14:10
Psalm 3
1 Corinthians 15:42-53

The reward of reading Torah portions is that it's easier to identify prophetic language embedded among the stories. For instance, when Jacob "sleeps," the reader should tune his or her channel to Death, and when he "awoke from his sleep," the channel should change to Resurrection.

Vayeitze is an especially mystical portion. Vayeitze means "when he went out" of the Promised Land. Jacob went into exile in Laban's land, Haran. His encounter with a Heavenly gate has an enduring connection to his descendants, the House of Judah and the House of Joseph. It is the prophecy of exile and return, not simply to the earthly Land of Israel, but to the spiritual realm of the Garden of Eden just above it.

The word makom ("place") is scattered multiple times in Jacob's encounter at Beit-El,[4] just as it is in the account of the binding of Isaac on Mount Moriah. "Makom" even occurs three times in one sentence, a resurrection marker:

> He came to a certain place and spent the night there, because the sun had set; and he took one of the stones of the place and put it under his head and lay down in that place.

Something a reader might miss is that there was an encounter even *before* Jacob dreamed his dream and realized where he was.

Although the English translation says Jacob "came" to the place, the Hebrew text reads much more specifically, *yifgah*. Yifgah means to encounter something, sometimes to touch the border of something or to meet with something. Yifgah is super-specific, not the generic English "came to." Jacob encountered or touched the border of something even before the dream that awakened him to the significance of the place. This is often the case when one goes to Israel. He or she may only realize what happened in hindsight. There was a Divine touch, as if the believer did touch a holy border in the journey.

> Then Jacob awoke from his sleep and said, 'Surely the LORD is in this place, and I did not know it.' He was afraid and said, 'How awesome is this place! This is none other than the house of God, and this is the gate of heaven.' So Jacob rose early in the morning, and took the stone that he had put under his head and set it up as a pillar and poured oil on its top. He called the name of that place Bethel; however, previously the name of the city had been Luz. Then

4. Bethel is a contraction of *beit* (house) + El (God). House of God.

> Jacob made a vow, saying, 'If God will be with me and will keep me on this journey that I take, and will give me food to eat and garments to wear, and I return to my father's house in safety, then the LORD will be my God. This stone, which I have set up as a pillar, will be God's house, and of all that You give me I will surely give a tenth to You.' (Ge 28:10-22)

The clue to the encounter is in the text. Jacob encountered Ha-makom, The Place, which specifically is the Temple Mount, the place of the House of El (God). The problem is that physically, Beit El is approximately eighteen miles from Jerusalem.

How those two locations may have merged is something of a textual mystery, but maybe not. In Scripture, it is not unusual for people to be "folded" into a different place in an encounter, such as Phillip from the Ethiopian's chariot[5] or Yeshua and his disciples from the middle of the Galilee to shore in an instant.[6] After he was taken by the Divine chariot, the local prophets searched for Elijah on the mountains even though Elisha assured them that he was gone.[7] In the days of the prophets, they didn't think it unusual for one of their own to be transported in space. Is it time travel or place travel? It would probably be necessary to see Jacob's ladder to know for certain.

Jacob's mission in exile was marriage. The promise in the dream was of "descendants," which was an affirmation of Jacob's journey. He was to find a godly wife and to father godly children. In order for him to do this, he encounters Ha-makom, The Place, which is...

> ...a gateway to heaven that spans the void between the physical terrain beneath his feet and the heavenly

5. Ac 8:27-40

6. Jn 6:21

7. 2 Ki 2:11-18

world, the spiritual and transcendent spheres beyond this world. Jacob's vision is almost unfathomable, for he describes spiritual structures that transcend the physical, yet have a physical manifestation. - (Kahn, p. 181-182)

To crack the security code to the gateway, the reader must return to the First Mention of makom:

> Then God said, 'Let the waters below the heavens be gathered into one place (makom), and let the dry land appear'; and it was so. (Ge 1:9)

The makom's first mention is in relation to the gathering of the waters "under the shamayim," or under heaven. Yeek-veh-u, or gathered, has the same root as mikveh, a ritual immersion for purity. One immerses after a touching the border of the realm of death and preparatory to entering the inner precincts of the "House."[8] Mikveh ("baptism" to Christians) is also "hope," and it makes sense why Yeshua immersed repentant people in a mikveh. He is their hope of being gathered into The Place, the House of El. He is their hope of producing fruits worthy of that repentance. He is their hope of resurrection.

8. A discharge of blood or childbirth were occasions for a mikveh for women; likewise, for men, an abnormal discharge or preparation for a high Sabbath are occasions for a mikveh. When examined, each situation represents a return from a life-threatening situation or purification from a deathly world before entering a holy place.

The gathering of water is the mikveh; the place of the gathering is ha-makom.

In Creation, the dry land emerges from the gathering of the place. Water is a symbol of spirit, so man emerges from the dust of the ground (Ge 2:7), a union of the spiritual and physical worlds. A very specific dust of the earth is used, earth that emerged from makom, the place. Connect the hints from the dust of "the place" Mount Moriah, the Temple Mount, and Beit-El, the House of El. Humankind (adam) was formed from the *adamah* (earth) of the House of God. Humankind was to bear the image of both the earthy and the heavenly, physical and spiritual, in a formed balance of precision. This explains the special role of the Temple Mount in humankind's unfolding history.

Targum Pseudo-Yonatan states that

> The dust was gathered from the place where the Beit HaMikdash [Temple] would stand. (*Targum Yonatan* to Bereishit 2:7)

That's shouting material if it's really sunk in. It explains why the heart longs to go to Israel, specifically, Jerusalem. You are not just a spiritual child of Jerusalem; your very physical body is derived from its earth! It is true, there's no makom like home...the House of Elohim.

When a believer is resurrected in Yeshua, the Mikveh Yisrael, Jacob's anointed "rock," his or her spirit *and* body want to turn homeward. Jacob's anointing of the oil on the pillar-rock is alluding to *mashiach*, or messiah, which means to be smeared or anointed with oil. Jacob's head rested on that rock while he "slept," figurative of death, but through that rock he will "arise early in the morning."

> When a believer returns to Jerusalem, he or she returns home in a very basic, elemental sense. The very stones of the Temple Mount are of one piece with our bodies. Human beings are part and parcel of the holy altar, and that holiest of places is intertwined with our very essence...exile is, above all, a disconnection from the source of our spiritual identity. (Kahn, 2011, pp. 185-186)

Jacob anoints the stone and sets it up as a pillar to mark the makom. He then departs to find his holy bride in the exile. He must produce godly descendants through a holy marriage. The word makom is related etymologically to mekayeim, something that sustains and provides existence. Perhaps this is why Abraham says to Sarah in Egypt (exile), "that I may live because of you."

There's No Makom Like Home

Jacob didn't depart for Haran immediately after his father's blessing. There are fourteen years missing in his life story, and Jewish tradition says Jacob served in the House of Eber, the descendant of Shem who passed on godly knowledge according to the priestly order of Malkhi-tzedek. The number fourteen is the generations of Messiah,[9] and Eber is from avar, the root of "Hebrew," one who has crossed or passed over.

The Torah prescribes that one who commits manslaughter must flee to a refuge city, a type of exile within the Land. His exile from his "place" ends with the death of the Cohen HaGadol. This suggests that symbolically, in Yeshua's passing into the heavens, those who believe in him are released from exile should they choose to return:

> Therefore, since we have a great high priest who has passed (Hebrew cognate: avar) through the heavens, Jesus the Son of God, let us hold fast our confession. (He 4:14)

9. As delineated in the Gospel genealogies.

10. In 2 Corinthians 12:2, Paul identifies Paradise, or the Garden of Eden, as the Third Heaven.

Although human beings are disconnected from their natural and spiritual makom in the third heaven[10] of the Garden of Eden, Yeshua has worked and continues working so that we, too, may be Hebrews and avar into the heavens. One typically thinks of going up into the heavens, but the Kingdom is also something to be crossed (avar) into.

Jacob is on his way into exile in Haran. He will need this perception of Ha-makom as God's House preparing for a holy bride in order to maintain his resolve to return. It also helps Jacob to focus on his job in exile: maintain his faith and marry a righteous bride. In his encounter at Beit-El, Jacob is reminded of the special dust from which he was formed, and his very physical being is part of that House of God:

> Or do you not know that your body is a temple of the Holy Spirit who is in you, whom you have from God, and that you are not your own? (1 Co 6:19)

Adonai assures Jacob that He will be with him both in exile and in his return to his place, his physical and spiritual source, the dust and water of the House of God.

> Our lives are bound up with the Altar in Jerusalem, with the dust of the earth of the Temple Mount. Every death, then is a destruction of the Altar and the Temple. (Kahn, p. 191)

This lends credence to John's reference in Revelation to the souls under the altar crying out. They are told to rest for a little while and given robes to wear[11] while they wait for the rest of the Body of Messiah. So, too, Jacob's vow involves invoking both bread and "garments to wear" in his exile. Two results of exile from Eden were lack of spiritual clothing and difficulty producing bread. Jacob also requests "return to my father's house." A return to the Garden. The Promised Land. My Father's House. HaMakom. To ascend and descend in order to guard and keep the spiritual and physical realms of earth according to Adam's original created nature.

At Luz, Jacob renames the "House of God" Beit-El. The mission of Jacob's "going out" is to find a wife,   11. Re 6:11

to make a holy marriage, not a Hittite marriage like Esau.

> He called the name of that place Bethel; however, previously the name of the city had been Luz [almond tree]. (Ge 28:19)

The original city-name of Luz is a clue. There was some way in which Luz touched the border or "met or reached" Ha-Makom, the Place of Moriah, the later Temple Mount.

When the tribes began conquering the Land of Israel and settling their tribal territory, Judah conquered Jerusalem with the "edge of the sword and set the city afire."[12] Later, there is an interruption to the Judges One narrative, which is describing activities of specific tribes. One would expect to read "Ephraim" or "Menashe,"[13] but instead, at the conquest of Beit-El, the writer inserts "House of Joseph":

> Likewise, the house of Joseph went up against Bethel, and the LORD was with them. The House of Joseph spied out Bethel (now the name of the city was formerly Luz). The spies saw a man coming out of the city and they said to him, 'Please show us the entrance to the city and we will treat you kindly.' So he showed them the entrance to the city, and they struck the city with the edge of the sword, but they let the man and all his family go free. The man went into the land of the Hittites and built a city and named it Luz, which is its name to this day. (Ju 1:22-26)

12. Ju 1:8
13. Manasseh

There a few more anomalies. If you see a man coming out of a city, why would you ask him to show you the entrance? It's either nonsensical or

24

prophetic, such as the men of Sodom not being able to find the door to Lot's house after the angels pulled him inside. No matter how blind a person is, he can find the doorway to a house in about five minutes... unless its concealment is supernatural. Something has folded, place or time. The unnamed man of Luz and his family moved north to the springs that feed into the Galilee. They built another city named Luz, which is still there.[14]

"Likewise, the House of Joseph went up against Bethel" means that Joseph succeeded also in conquering a separate area known as Beit-El, just as Judah conquered Jerusalem. But the grammar suggests more. The House of Joseph *also* went up to Beit-El. As Judah went up, so did the House of Joseph. The use of the word *ya-alu*, "went up," symbolizes resurrection. Like an *olah* offering from the same root, it means to ascend into the heavens.

So there are two possibilities. The House of Joseph conquered a separate area about eighteen miles north of Jerusalem after Judah conquered Jerusalem. But what if the "man" they encountered coming out of an entrance, whom they could see in the physical realm, represents a "meeting" of Jerusalem and Beit-El, like Jacob's, when the text also makes sure the reader knows the original name of the city was Luz?

This language teases with resurrection like Jacob's encounter with the entrance to Heaven. Perhaps the wording is folding together two separate locations into one, just as rabbinic commentary speculates. They say that Moriah was folded into Beit-El so that Jacob could pray at the chosen place of his father's Isaac's self-sacrifice. It would be space-bending, or in this case, place-bending, to encourage the House of Joseph. It may be a prophecy concerning the ability of the House of Joseph to do as Judah had done, to find and gain entrance to Jerusalem, the House and "the place"

14. See the village in Lebanon, Louaize, just on the border of Lebanon and Israel.

of El.

> Thus says the LORD, 'Yet again
> there will be heard in this place,
> of which you say, "It is a waste,
> without man (adam) and without
> beast," that is, in the cities of Judah
> and in the streets of Jerusalem that
> are desolate, without man (adam)
> and without inhabitant (yoshev)
> and without beast, the voice of
> joy and the voice of gladness, the
> voice of the bridegroom and the
> voice of the bride, the voice of those
> who say, "Give thanks to the LORD
> of hosts, for the LORD is good, for His
> lovingkindness is everlasting"; and of
> those who bring a thank offering
> into the house of the LORD. For I will
> restore the fortunes of the land as
> they were at first,' says the LORD. (Je
> 33:10-12)

Without human beings to "be fruitful and multiply" in
Ha-makom in Eden, and with the fall of the animal
kingdom with them, the planted Garden was
empty. Ultimately, Yeshua's mission was to restore
the Bride to the Garden so that joy and gladness
would once again be heard there, "as they were at
first" at the first marriage. Jacob was ordered to do
this by his parents and sent into exile.

Rabbi Nachman says that the angels who Jacob
saw "going up and coming down" were dancing
at the entrance. Dancing is still an important part
of marriage ceremonies. The angels danced for
Jacob's journey to make a holy family in exile. They
danced for his plan to return and build a Holy House
on earth to bring offerings. (Kahn, p. 208)

> R. Helbo said: 'Whoever enjoys the
> wedding meal of a bridegroom

and does not help him to rejoice transgresses against the five voices mentioned in the verse':

"'The voice of joy and the voice of gladness, the voice of the bridegroom and the voice of the bride, the voice of those who shall say, 'Give thanks to the Lord of Hosts.'" (Je 33:11)

And if one helps the Bridegroom to rejoice, it is as if he restored one of the ruins of Jerusalem. (*Talmud Bavli Brachot 6b*)

Marrying a holy spouse or rejoicing with the bride and bridegroom are counted as a thank-offering to the Temple in Jerusalem. It's the angels' ladder-dance...and the latter-day dance.

Jacob connects to his son Joseph with "Luz" when it is time to bless the House of Joseph, Ephraim and Menashe, in Genesis 48:3-8:

Then Jacob said to Joseph, 'God Almighty appeared to me *at Luz* in the land of Canaan and blessed me, and He said to me, "'Behold, I will make you fruitful and numerous...'"

Isaac's blessing on Jacob...God Almighty's blessing on Jacob...Jacob's blessing on the House of Joseph... all connected to help the House of Joseph also find their way from exile to the entrance to Jerusalem, and this time, to dwell there. The "man" who built the new Luz built on the spring that starts the water-flow into the Galilee. From there, the water flows into the Yarden (Jordan), and then into the Dead Sea. Luz is an almond tree, the representation of the menorah, adorned with almond blossoms.

Now when I had returned, behold, on

the bank of the river there were very many trees on the one side and on the other. Then he said to me, 'These waters go out toward the eastern region and go down into the Arabah; then they go toward the sea, being made to flow into the sea, and the waters of the sea become fresh. It will come about that every living creature which swarms in every place where the river goes, will live. And there will be very many fish, for these waters go there and the others become fresh; so everything will live where the river goes. And it will come about that fishermen will stand beside it; from Engedi to Eneglaim there will be a place for the spreading of nets. Their fish will be according to their kinds, like the fish of the Great Sea, very many. But its swamps and marshes will not become fresh; they will be left for salt. By the river on its bank, on one side and on the other, will grow all kinds of trees for food. Their leaves will not wither and their fruit will not fail. They will bear every month because their water flows from the sanctuary, and their fruit will be for food and their leaves for healing.' (Ezek 47:7-12)

The Galilee is shaped like a harp. From the tiny spring of resurrection at Luz, through the harp of the Galilee, to the beginning of mankind, Beth-El, the place of the Temple Mount, then south to the Dead Sea, the song of resurrection will flow through the river. The Dead Sea will be brought to life, and every living creature which swarms in every place where the river goes will live.

It is not coincidence that Yeshua was immersed at the area where the Yarden, which means "descending," merges into the Dead Sea. From a dead collection of waters, Yeshua ascended to proclaim he was the River of Life that came down, and he will return again from Heaven to descend for his Bride. Israel will at the same time ascend at the resurrection from the Dead Sea. Two realms meet again. All Israel will find the entrance to Jerusalem above and be restored to their Garden, a spiritual and a holy natural creation married...and the angels will dance.

Louaize, Lebanon

The Sea of Galilee

The Dead Sea

THE SECRET SONG OF THE FROGS IN THE OVEN

Va'era "and appeared"
Exodus 6:2-9:35
Ezekiel 28:25-29:21
Psalm 46
Revelation 16:3-7; Matthew 10:22-33

As cute as a frog is sitting on a lily pad, you wouldn't want him in your bed or your oven. The plagues weren't fun for anyone.

The ancient sages ask, "If I AM could just remove Israel from Egypt, why didn't He? Why go through ten plagues first?" There is a theological purpose to the plagues. It is a vital part to forming a collective and personal concept of salvation. Without the plagues, Israel's understanding of Adonai would be insufficient. The sages say that the purpose of the plagues was to establish the truth of God's existence. It was experiential. *Knowing* for sure. It separated the truth of ONE from Pharaoh's lies of divinity and more than 2,000 Egyptian gods.

- If the Israelites didn't *know* Him, through pressure, they would.

- If Pharaoh didn't *know* Him, through pressure, he would.
- If the Egyptians and mixed multitude didn't *know* Him, through pressure, they would.

"To know" in Hebrew is found in its root *yada*, is to have experiential knowledge. It can be a positive experience, or it can be a painful experience, yet it is an experience. It is more than just information about some deity, it is a revelation of power. A group of rabbis once debated: "Which is better, Torah study or actions?"

The conclusion was that study was better because it *led to* appropriate action. Without study, the action could be erroneous, misapplied because it was misunderstood. The context of these rabbis' debate paints it in much more vivid colors. The rabbis risked their lives to have this Torah debate. They were hiding in an attic. Like the Egyptians and Greeks before them, the Romans had virtually cut off all Torah study, especially in public. Public displays of faith could get them crucified, scourged, skin removed with iron combs, etc.

The rabbis' clandestine debate included one of the *mitzvot* of Passover:

> Each generation is to engage the telling of the Exodus as if he or she, personally, experienced it.

Passover is not just a story, not just a debate over what one should have on the *seder* plate, not just a matter of selecting the right *haggadah*. You were there. *You* must feel the pressure of the government's desire to kill you because you believe Moses and desire to celebrate a feast to worship the one God of Abraham, Isaac, and Jacob alone. "Were you there?" asks the old spiritual song. "Were you there when they crucified my Lord?" Yes, *you* were.

At the Passover seder, in the midst of all the fun and food, in telling the story, the tellers must feel the pressure. What did it feel like for a Hebrew? How terrified must they have been, especially when they suffered from the first plagues along with the Egyptians! And this was after months of extra-hard labor and beatings to collect their own straw and the order of infanticide. So many tribulations.

Backing up a bit, first, Moses gave Pharaoh a sign. Moses threw down his staff, and it turned into a snake. Although the reader focuses on the magicians' ability to duplicate the sign, also turning their staffs into serpents, think about that. A serpent introduced sin and *death* into humankind. If Pharaoh was truly Divine, shouldn't his response have been like Moses' second sign, having his serpents *swallow* Moses' serpent? If Pharaoh was the "great crocodile" as he purported,[15] giving life to Egypt through his domain, the Nile, then he should be able to devour Moses' creation!

All Pharaoh's magicians could do was introduce more sin and death into the world, for Egypt represents Sheol, Abaddon, death, and the grave. Pharaoh commanded the magicians to make more snakes. Maybe it was just an oversight on Pharaoh's part. He forgot he was supposed to be god.

Pharaoh should probably head-smack at this point.

Then Moses turns the Nile into blood. Here's Pharaoh's chance to prove he's a god, the creator of the Nile. Pharaoh was a bit like the politician who purported that he invented the internet. Pharaoh "invented" the Nile...or so it was believed. So if Pharaoh created the Nile, then why could Moses turn it to blood and death, but Pharaoh couldn't return it to life? All Pharaoh could do was to have

5. One of the verses uses "*tanin*," for crocodile instead of *nachash*, for serpent.

his magicians mimic the miracle and produce more blood. Seriously, Pharaoh? The proper miracle would have been to transform the river from death to life, to clear away the blood. Instead, Pharaoh wants more death.

Wrong miracle, Pharaoh. Another head-smack.

It's not a magic competition. It's so *all* will "*know* that there is no one like the LORD our God."[16] If Pharaoh was really the god of the Nile, then his subjects could see him bleeding out, not making his realm healthy. The Egyptians grew tired over a week of seeking living water in muddy, bloody puddles. Pharaoh could not create living water. There was probably lots of head-smacking going on in Egypt.

After blood comes frogs. The frogs spread through Egypt. Everywhere. There are millions of stinking frogs, and Pharaoh's choice of miracles is...more frogs. You know what to do, Pharaoh (head-smack). At this point, the Egyptians must have been suffering from killer headaches as well.

> Then Pharaoh called for Moses and Aaron and said, 'Entreat the LORD that He remove the frogs from me and from my people; and I will let the people go, that they may sacrifice to the LORD.' Moses said to Pharaoh, 'The honor is yours to tell me: when shall I entreat for you and your servants and your people, that the frogs be destroyed from you and your houses, *that they may be left only in the Nile?*'

> Then he said, 'Tomorrow.' So he said, 'May it be according to your word, *that you may know that there is no one like the LORD our God. The frogs will depart from you and your*

16. Ex 8:10

34

houses and your servants and your people; *they will be left only in the Nile.*' Then Moses and Aaron went out from Pharaoh, and Moses cried to the LORD concerning the frogs which He had inflicted upon Pharaoh. The LORD did according to the word of Moses, and the frogs died out of the houses, the courts, and the fields. So they piled them in heaps, and the land became foul. (Ex 8:8-14)

So there were two types of frogs. The dead ones and the living ones in the Nile. The living ones in the Nile are symbolic. The Nile is the physical representation of the Pishon River,[17] the outermost of the encircling rivers of Eden. The frogs who left the river eventually had to die, just like Adam and Eve. The frogs who stayed in their natural habitat, the habitation of Divine design, would live.

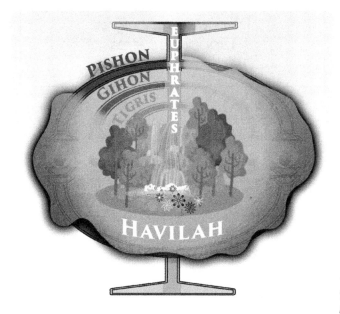

17. Pishon is said to represent *pishton*, or flax, which grows beside the Nile.

Watching Pharaoh's response to Moses must have been like watching politics today. The longer you watch, the more you say, "If these are the people in charge, things can only get worse."

And then they do.

Maybe instead of making more frogs, Pharaoh's magicians should have tried making them go back into the Nile to sing their proper song. Take a frog out of the water, and it's only a matter of time until it dies. A singing frog has a special job to do, and it is done at appointed times. Anytime is okay to a bullfrog, but not a singing frog. They are Divinely programmed for the music to start and stop. Listen, and you'll hear it. A frog sounds like a bird at night. [18]

Frogs sing a hidden song, and it is a song Bible-readers already know. Maybe you sing it every day. First, though, think about what a frog symbolizes:

> Tzfardea, Frog = צְפַרְדֵּעַ
> Tzippor, Bird = צִפֹּר
> De'a, Knowledge = דֵּעַ

A frog is a "bird of knowledge." It was knowledge that caused Adam and Eve to depart from the Garden River Pishon:

> Now the man called his wife's name Eve, because she was the mother of all the living. *The LORD God made garments of skin* for Adam and his wife, and *clothed them*. Then the LORD God said, 'Behold, the man has become like one of Us, *knowing* (*yada*) good and evil; and now, he might stretch out his hand, and take also from the tree of life, and eat, and live forever' - therefore the LORD

God sent him out from the garden of
Eden, to cultivate the ground from
which he was taken. (Ge 3:20-23)

Adam and Eve did not "keep," or guard, their
garments. They mixed the de'a of good and evil;
therefore, they were naked, unprepared for Elohim
to visit them in the Garden. Their souls could "fly"
like a bird back and forth in the Garden until they
believed and acted upon a lie. Afterward, they
fell, or descended to mere natural earth. No more
moving back and forth.

Who are these who fly like a cloud
and like the doves to their lattices? (Is
60:8)

Yeshua came to restore humankind's power to fly
back into the Garden with his great altar sacrifice of
resurrection. He was an excellent example of how
at first, Adam and Eve might have moved in and out
of spiritual and natural realms as if it were no barrier
at all, nothing hidden. Yeshua could walk on water,
hide himself in a crowd, or move from one place to
another in a moment. He even let Peter, James, and
John try out their "wings" by letting them see into a
makom out of time on the mount of transfiguration.
They were able to see Moses and Elijah, alive and
talking.

While believers wait, they are commanded, "keep
your garments." In other words, remove the de'a of
evil in a continuous guarding and evaluation
process. It's work. It's building Garden skills. The
Biblical feasts and sabbaths help Israel to reflect on
her work, for the feasts flowed from the River of Life
from the Throne. The lowly frog knows it, and it sings
this secret. A frog's water-song reminds Israel that
although frogs can't fly, and neither can human
beings, someday the resurrected dead will fly.[19] It
was prophesied on the Fifth Day of Creation when
the birds were created. It corresponds to the fifth

feast, the Feast of Trumpets, Yom Teruah, when those who have kept their garments will go up like birds to their nesting-place.

When "the LORD God sent him out from the garden of Eden, to cultivate the ground from which he was taken," Adam fathered children who would return to the physical place of the Garden. There they would build a Temple, a holy place worthy for the upper, spiritual garden to descend and once again "marry" the two realms. Those who are Jerusalem would ascend, or *ya-alu* like an *olah* sacrifice, and the spiritual Jerusalem would descend *yarad* like the Yarden River. Yeshua was buried in a garden in Jerusalem, demonstrating that a place of death was once again accessible as a place of life.

One of the rabbis who hid while debating whether study or action was more important was Rabbi Akiva. He made a terrible mistake when he believed that Bar-Kokhba was the Messiah, and he knew it. Rabbi Akiva came out of hiding and began gathering students to teach Torah. He was captured by the Romans and martyred for teaching. He was skinned alive with iron combs, and he died while reciting the Shema.

Many Jews flocked to Bar Kokhba, a false messiah, and they were killed. On the other hand, Rabbi Akiva's martyrdom sparked a great fervor for Torah study, his students having witnessed his manner of death, saying the Shema and drawing out the word "*echad*" in "God is *One*," so he would die with it on his lips. Rabbi Akiva was the one who said study comes before action. He realized that he had to put his belief into action. Merely believing someone is Messiah is one thing; do we believe it enough to sacrifice our own lives for that belief? Whether this was Rabbi Akiva's act of repentance for his error is a question for the True Judge Himself.

19. Ps 124:7 The sacrifice of one's life was another topic of

these famous Passover attic-debaters. Rabbi Akiva represents the potential of the frog. On the one hand, it can be a false prophet. On the other hand, it can sing the song of martyrdom for the unity of the Name in the greatest commandment, the Shema. It was in the same attic[20] that Torah teachers discussed under what conditions martyrdom for the Torah was required. They concluded idolatry, sexual licentiousness, and murder. One should choose death over these sins if necessary.

There is an older example of the frog martyrdom dilemma. Moses told Pharaoh:

> The Nile will swarm with frogs, which will come up and go into your house and into your bedroom and on your bed, and into the houses of your servants and on your people, and **into your ovens** and into your kneading bowls. So the frogs will come up on you and your people and all your servants. (Ex 8:1-4)

"Into your ovens" is a strange location. A swarm of frogs might hop into an open kneading bowl or on top of a bed, but into a hot oven? The frogs obeyed a Divine command to commit suicide. (We're not advocating suicide here...head-smack). Consistent with Passover as a time for Israel to contemplate the cost of serving and worshiping YHVH, the frogs leap into hot ovens to serve their Creator with their body and soul. Because it hints at a bird-like quality, the frogs "went up," or *alah*, symbolizing one's very soul ready to ascend if called upon to commit idolatry, sexual immorality, or murder.

According to one rabbi, the courage of the frogs inspired three men to face the oven likewise: Shadrach, Meshach, and Abed-nego of Daniel 3:8-30. In spite of their trembling at their situation, the Jewish wise men kept their garments in the midst of the

20. Sanhedrin 74a

fire. Garments of obedience don't burn in Heavenly rivers, and they didn't even smell of smoke! The One True King is able to help the righteous to cross the burning Rivers of Eden. In that day, it is the wicked who burn without garments of salvation. The three... no four...one like the Son of God...would not worship an idol.

Putting belief into action may cause death, but it is life. The fires that really count are the burning Rivers of Eden, for the definition of a river[21] in Hebrew is something "burning and shining." Yeshua stood at Sukkot[22] and said he was the source of river waters for the "thirsty," a characteristic of the dead rich man in Yeshua's parable of death. To those in Yeshua's hand, the fire is not harmful, but a return to the life of home in the Garden. They drink from the rivers of the Spirit.

> The angel of the LORD appeared to him in a blazing fire from the midst of a bush; and he looked, and behold, the bush was burning with fire, yet the bush was not consumed. (Ex 3:2)

> Do not fear those who kill the body but are unable to kill the soul; but rather fear Him who is able to destroy both soul and body in hell. (Mt 10:28)

Passover is to experience the Holy One. You were there, and you are here.

The frog-song of Passover is a reminder of martyrdom. What would a believer endure to obey a commandment? Many people have heard a whistle calling them to the Torah. Without seeing the frog as both a "knowledgeable bird" and a martyr for the knowledge of the Word, those who hear the whistle are in grave danger.

21. *nahar*
22. Jn 7:37-39

The danger is that believers will become so engrossed in the details, they will forget to get up and go practice it. It will be reduced to analysis and correction, but there will be none willing to live at frog level. If a frog can obey a commandment to jump in an oven, then someone who is called to the Torah must be willing to sacrifice something for it without complaining.

Knowledgeable frog-birds must allow themselves to be pulled from the comfort zone to obey a commandment for a very specific reason: so that Pharaoh and the Egyptians will KNOW that there is One True Creator and King in Israel and in the fiery furnace of affliction. Egypt is Abaddon.[23] The pharaohs can only produce more death and misery. The God of Israel plucks life from death. He returns the repentant captives to the living Rivers of Eden; He removes the blood from the water; He swallows up death and sin in victory.

The Hebrews were *already* afraid even before the plagues started. They were already trembling. Imagine having blood and frogs piled on top, before the "finger of God"[24] made a distinction between His people and the Egyptians. To echo a modern tribulation, people were *already* afraid even before the plagues like COVID-19 and economic collapse struck the world. They feared government conspiracies, MSG in their food, rising violence, GMO, too much immigration, too little immigration...

Even in the study of Torah, believers sit and tremble at the world around them. They tremble even *before* someone comes to take our lives. If the plagues are the "finger of God" as even Pharaoh's servants pointed out, then perhaps the plague serves a dual function. Perhaps His finger is to pry *believers'* fingers from the systems in which they trust: politics, government, health care, weapons, the stock market, etc.

23. "Pharaoh's servants said to him, 'How long will this man be a snare to us? Let the men go, that they may serve the LORD their God. Do you not realize that Egypt is *destroyed (avdah)*?'" Abaddon is the permanent construct and realm of *avdah*, or destruction, ruin. Go to www.thecreationgospel.com archived newsletters and read "Don't You Know Egypt is Abaddon?" for a full explanation of Egypt as Abaddon.

24. Ex 8:19

If one is afraid in the element in which he lives, how much more in the element in which he would die! So it is with us. If such is our condition when we sit and study the Torah, of which it is written, "For that is your life and the length of your days,"[25] if we go and neglect it, how much worse off we shall be![26]

R' Kahn writes:

> Study is great, theory is important, philosophy is necessary, but it must eventually lead to practice. There is a time to theorize, a time to debate and cast votes, and there is a time to act, to carry one's convictions through to fruition. (2012, p. 48)

It's easy for the frog to sing in the river. What if he's called to sing throughout Egypt? Will he do it? Will we do it?

> And I saw coming out of the mouth of the dragon and out of the mouth of the beast and out of the mouth of the false prophet, three unclean spirits *like* frogs; for they are spirits of demons, performing signs, which go out to the kings of the whole world, to gather them together for the war of the great day of God, the Almighty. Behold, I am coming like a thief. *Blessed is the one who stays awake and keeps his clothes, so that he will not walk about naked and men will not see his shame.* And they gathered them together to the place which in Hebrew is called Har-Magedon. (Re 16:13-16)

25. Dt 30:20

26. *Talmud Bavli Berakhot 61b*

There will be fake frogs sent forth as false prophets. They are only LIKE the singing frogs. It's one thing to study Torah, and it is another to "stay awake" and "guard" one's clothes, which requires more than study. It requires DOING that which one studies and believes. Clothes are deeds. Failing to guard the precepts of the Garden here is one way to remain bare of honorable clothes at the resurrection. Faith without works is *dead*. One who has not been diligent in study will not be diligent in action. A frog out of the River.

The truthful, knowledgeable frogs sing to Israel every feast, every Shabbat, from every Passover Spring to every Autumn Sukkot during the season of the moedim. When country folks hear the singing frogs, spring is near. When their song fades away, winter is coming. According to *Perek Shira*, a work traditionally ascribed to King David, the frog's song is "BLESSED BE THE NAME OF HIS GLORIOUS KINGDOM FOREVER AND EVER." It is taken from King David's final song, the Eighth Song of prophecy[27]:

> May his name endure forever; may His name increase as long as the sun shines; and let men bless themselves by Him; let all nations call Him blessed. Blessed be *the LORD God, the God of Israel, Who alone works wonders. And blessed be His glorious name forever*; and may the whole earth be filled with His glory. Amen, and Amen. The prayers of David the son of Jesse are ended. (Ps 72:17-20)

In the Jewish daily prayers, the "frog" phrase is inserted between the first line of the Shema, the greatest commandment: "Hear, O Israel, the LORD your God, the LORD is One" and the rest of the proclamation, "...and you shall love the LORD your God with all your heart, all your soul, and with all your might..."

In the original frog-n-prince story, the frog was

27. The Ten Songs of prophecy will be listed in the next chapter.

43

created to begin his song at the time of the evening Shema and to cease at the morning Shema. It is the verse of praise inserted between the first sentence of the Shema, which declares there is only One, and the first paragraph, which contains the obligation to love God with all one's heart, soul, and resources, even unto death. It is sung in the darkness, a light that shines when all the Egyptians have is darkness. Jewish tradition says that when the Gentiles start to sing the Shema, that full redemption, the Messiah, is near.

The dragon, beast, and false prophet can only be "like" a real frog. They could never bring themselves to proclaim, love, or serve the ONE Elohim, Creator of the Universe. Their signs are all false, their resurrections never permanent or to very goodness. They are death, not life.

And now you know the secret song the frog-bird sings at night:

> Blessed be His glorious Name forever
> And ever and ever and ever and ever and ever...

Sing, Children, Sing!

The Shema

Hear, O Israel, the LORD is our God, the LORD is
One.

(*Shema, Yisrael, Adonai, Eloheynu, Adonai Echad*)

Blessed is the name of His glorious kingdom for all
eternity.

(*Baruch shem kvod, malkhuto, l'olam va-ed.*)

And you shall love the LORD your God with all your
heart, with all your soul, and with all your might.
And have these words, which I command you this
day, be upon your heart. And you shall teach them
diligently to your children, and speak of them when
you sit in your house, when you walk by the way,
when you retire, and when you arise. And you shall
bind them for a sign upon your hand and let them
be frontlets between your eyes. And you shall write
them on the doorposts of your house and on your
gates.

3

THE SONG OF MOSES

Haazinu "Give ear"
Deuteronomy 32:1-32:52
2 Samuel 22:1-51
Psalm 71
John 5:24

The Song of Moses at the Sea of Reeds (Red Sea) is not the Song of Moses, but perhaps the proto-Song of Moses. Re-sung in numerous praise and worship songs, the Song of Moses is not nearly as comforting, at least in its beginning, as the Song of the Sea. It is more ominous in its prophecies, and the very name of the Torah portion *Haazinu* is repeated numerous times in the Book of Revelation and especially in Yeshua's sermons. "Give ear" and "He who has an ear, let him hear" are flashing red signals pointing the reader to the Song of Moses, Haazinu.

Two Witnesses

Moses silenced Heaven and Earth to become witnesses to his song:

> Give ear, O heavens, and let me speak; and let the earth hear the words of my mouth. (Dt 32:1)

There are other silences that parallel it, but Revelation also records that there will be a silence:

> When the Lamb broke the seventh seal, there was silence in heaven for about half an hour. (Re 8:1)

Half an hour would be sufficient time for the parasha Haazinu[28] to be sung or chanted in most synagogues. Moses calls on two important witnesses, Heaven and Earth. Each has its song from the time of creation. Look up into the Heavens on a beautiful, starry night, and you may hear it:

> The heavens are telling of the glory of God; and their expanse is declaring the work of His hands.
> (Ps 19:1)

And the Earth's song is this:

> The earth is the LORD'S, and all it contains, the world, and those who dwell in it. From the ends of the earth we hear songs, 'Glory to the Righteous One.' (Is 24:16)

These are two faithful witnesses created to perform the will of the Creator. They proclaim that He alone is their Creator, and they have been His witnesses from the beginning of the creation of Heaven and Earth.

In the Jewish tradition, a song, or *shir*, is therefore defined as:

1. The performance of God's will
2. Recognition that He and He alone is the Master of the heavenly and earthly regions, and that He and He alone is to be feared, loved, and served. (*Perek Shirah*, p. 12)

28. A complete investigation and explication of the Song of Moses is located in *Creation Gospel Workbook Two* by the author. There is a complete chart correlating the Song of Moses with the Book of Revelation.

Although there are many songs in the Scriptures, and many words for different types of songs and poems, there are Ten Songs recognized as having a prophetic identity. They fall within the definition of a *shir*, or *shirah*, which is to perform God's will and recognize Him alone as the Master of Heavenly and Earthly regions.

1. Adam recited the first shirah in the Garden of Eden for the Shabbat: "*Mizmor shir leyom HaShabbat*," [29] in which he praised the greatness of Shabbat and prophesied of restoration.
2. At the miraculous crossing of the Reed Sea, Israel sang a shirah.
3. Israel sang a shirah for Miriam's well.
4. Moses taught Haazinu, the Song of Moses, on the day of his death.
5. When Joshua fought the Amorites, he ordered the sun to stop, so he sang its shirah[30] of praise while it was silent from performing its full work.
6. Deborah composed a shirah when Adonai defeated Sisera and his army.
7. Chana gave birth to Samuel and sang a shirah.
8. King David sang a shirah at the end of his life (2 Sa 22)
9. King Solomon wrote Shir HaShirim, Song of Songs.
10. The Tenth Song will be sung by Israel when God redeems them from the present exile. (Re 14:3) It is the song of Messiah.[31]

29. Psalm 92; see the full psalm at the end of this chapter.

30. The sun sings: "Sun and moon stood in their places; they went away at the light of Your arrows, at the radiance of Your gleaming spear." (Ha 3:11; Joshua 10:12-13); The moon sings: "He made the moon for festivals; the sun knows its destination." (Ps 104:19)

31. Tanchuma Beshalach 10; Shir HaShirim Zuta 1:1

The Tenth Song is of particular interest because it has not yet been sung. There is yet much prophecy to be fulfilled until the singing of that song. John hints to it in Revelation, but he records by name his vision of the Song of Moses:

> And they *sang* the *Song of Moses*, the bond-servant of God, and the song

of the Lamb, saying... (Re 15:3)

The Greek word for "sang" in Revelation 15:3 is cognate to the root *shur*, which forms the noun for *shirah*. It can also mean a chant. The Hebrew Scriptures are all chanted. The appearance of both Haazinu, the Fourth Song, and the song of Messiah, the Tenth Song, in Revelation affirms the rabbinic principle that these prophetic songs were layered.

For instance, the Song of Songs contains elements of previous songs. The *Midrash Rabbah* to Haazinu states something that should sound familiar to any reader of Revelation as it concerns the two "witnesses," also described as the two olive trees and the two lampstands:

> These have the power to shut up the sky, so that rain will not fall during the days of their prophesying; and they have power over the waters to turn them into blood, and to strike the earth with every plague, as often as they desire. (Re 11:6)

These two witnesses have power over the rain of heaven and over the waters and earth with blood and plague. There are more than two witnesses. There are two witnesses, Heaven and Earth, to the two witnesses.

The Two Witnesses of the Two Witnesses

John's vision is very close to the ancient Jewish sages' view of the end of days.

> Great tzaddikim [righteous people] are able to reverse the laws of nature: The prophet Eliyahu [Elijah] turned winter, the rainy season, into summer. He promised, 'I swear there will be rain and dew according to my

word.' (1 Ki 17:1) A drought then set in to punish the Jews for worshiping idols. (*The Midrash Says* to Haazinu, p. 349)

While the Heavens and Earth were two witnesses to the Shirah, they were witnesses to Moses, the one who had the power to turn water into blood and bring down plagues; the prophet Elijah shut up the sky. The two witnesses described by John are based in Jerusalem. The Midrash asks,

> Why does G-d give tzaddikim the power to change laws of nature? So that people should fear them and thereby begin to fear Hashem. (ibid)

This is *exactly* the definition of a shir. The two faithful witnesses in Revelation are given power to change the laws of nature in order to bring the people of the earth to acknowledge their Creator and to reverence Him. To reverence Him is to have the Spirit of Reverence, the *Yirat Adonai*. When one reverences Adonai, then he or she will perform His will and obey Him. He or she will sing His songs.

The First Song, the Song of the Sabbath Day, Psalm 92, was composed for the seventh day of Creation. Overlay the seven spirits of Adonai as listed in Isaiah 11:2-3, and the seventh spirit is Yirat Adonai, or the The Spirit of Reverence (Fear) of Adonai. Psalm 92 contains the two elements of a shir, the acknowledgment of the Creator as the only One who is to be served, and the performance of His will:

> But You, O LORD, are on high forever.
> (verse 8)
> They [the righteous] will still yield fruit
> in old age. (verse 14)

Just prior to the singing of the Second Song, the Song at the Sea, Moses tells the Israelites to stand still and see the "Yeshuat" of Adonai. The people are terrified of the Egyptian chariots racing toward them. They are hemmed in by the Reed Sea. Rather than panic, Moses says to be still, just as there is a half-hour of silence in Heaven in Revelation.

In Biblical thinking, silence is affirmation![32] Silence says Israel agrees with the work of the Holy One and His Yeshuat (salvation). That stillness at the Sea of Reeds precedes their shirah of deliverance, the Second Song, which explains the stillness prior to the opening of the Seventh Seal in Revelation. It is silent affirmation of Yeshua. By adding the Hebrew letter tav[33] at the end of the word Yeshua, it makes it possessive; in other words, "the salvation of Adonai," therefore, Yeshuat.

Here is another example:

yireh - reverence, respect, fear
Yirat Adonai - the reverence of Adonai

The first great song of Israel, the Second Song, came after the splitting of the Reed Sea in Exodus 15. The preamble describes the spiritual condition that preceded the song:

> ...and the people revered the LORD, and they had faith in the LORD and in Moses, His servant. (Ex 14:31)

The death and resurrection of the two witnesses, and the earthquake that follows, brings the intended result of the witnesses' signs:

> And in that hour there was a great earthquake, and a tenth of the city fell; seven thousand people were killed in the earthquake, and the rest were terrified [Gr. emphobos= He. yirat] and gave glory to the God of heaven. (Re 11:13)

32. Nu 30:11

33. Tav ת sounds like the English t.

52

At last, a song in the Holy City! Reverence accomplished! In Revelation Chapter 15, the righteous sing the Shirah of Moses. In their proclamation of the Word, the two witnesses demonstrate that Moses' two witnesses have become the executioners of the Song. Heaven and earth bear witness that the Torah will drop like rain and flow like dew. The famine, plagues, and fires break out from Heaven and Earth to bring about the final redemption of the righteous. Heaven and Earth sing their shirim:

> The sun sings: 'Sun and moon stood in their places; they went away at the light of Your arrows, at the radiance of Your gleaming spear.' (Ha 3:11; Joshua 10:12-13); The moon sings: 'He made the moon for festivals; the sun knows its destination.' (Ps 104:19)

The two witnesses have two witnesses, Heaven and Earth. The two witnesses also turn into executioners of the judgments, their "hands" being the first to act with famine (Heaven), plague (Earth).

> But you shall surely kill him; your hand shall be first against him to put him to death, and afterwards the hand of all the people. So you shall stone him to death because he has sought to seduce you from the LORD your God who brought you out from the land of Egypt, out of the house of slavery. Then all Israel will hear and be afraid, and will never again do such a wicked thing among you. (Dt 13:9-11)

The two witnesses are "watched" when they resurrect into the cloud:

> And their dead bodies will lie in the street of the great city which

mystically is called Sodom and Egypt, where also their Lord was crucified. *Those from the peoples and tribes and tongues and nations will look at their dead bodies for three and a half days and will not permit their dead bodies to be laid in a tomb.* And those who dwell on the earth will rejoice over them and celebrate; and they will send gifts to one another, because these two prophets tormented those who dwell on the earth. But after the three and a half days, the breath of life from God came into them, and they stood on their feet; and great fear fell upon those who were watching them. And they heard a loud voice from heaven saying to them, "Come up here." Then they went up into heaven in the cloud, *and their enemies watched them.* (Re 11:8-12)

The tradition says that the Israelites were protected in the wilderness with seven Clouds of Glory, carrying them on the wings of an eagle and caring for them "like an eagle stirs up its nest." In Deuteronomy 32:1-11, Rahab says the nations were aware of Israel's Divine protection; they "watched" them.

When they walked in the same reverence as at the Song of the Sea, the clouds gave the Israelites a semi-resurrected travel experience. The events of Revelation are to restore reverence in the Earth and its songs witness to "the performance of God's will and that He alone is to be feared, loved, and served." The Creation was brought about by the Word, and it will be resurrected by the Word:

Haazinu gives us the most explicit statement of the resurrection in the Torah:

> And there is no god besides Me; it
> is I who put to death and give life. I
> have wounded and it is I who heal...
> (Dt 32:39)

Which sums up the definition of shirah. In Revelation, there are "books" which define one's position, either of Yirat or death. Notice the pattern of Adonai's work:

Put to Death ➔ give life
Wound ➔ heal

With the Word, Creation came to life. By the Word, it died. By the Word, it was wounded. By the Word, it will be healed. The Tree of Life is for the healing of the nations. The Song of Moses gives the details of the "performance of God's will" through words, speech.

> Give ear, O heavens, and let me
> speak; and let the earth hear the
> words of my mouth. Let my teaching
> drop as the rain, my speech distill as
> the dew, as the droplets on the fresh
> grass and as the showers on the herb.
> For I proclaim the name of the LORD;
> ascribe greatness to our God! (Dt
> 32:1-3)

The Midrash to verse 39 says:

Our Sages explain even though the human body decays after death, the soul continues to exist in the eternal world of life. The souls of tzaddikim and tzidkanyot [righteous men and women] experience tremendous enjoyment and bliss. The greater their spiritual achievements in this world, the more intense the bliss after death. The world which these souls enter after death is usually referred to as Gan Eden. [34]

The Midrash goes on to show the division of mankind's existence, which is very close to Revelation's (20:4-6) division of eras: "We may divide mankind's existence into five periods."[35]

1. Life in the present world.
2. Gan Eden, where souls of the righteous are stored until *techiat ha-metim*, the resurrection.
3. The era of Mashiach.
4. *Techiat ha-metim*, when God restores the dead to life with what the Sages call the 'dew of revival.' The period will be preceded by the Great Day of Judgment, about which Daniel prophesied (12:2).
5. The Olam Haba, or the World to Come.

The *Techiat Ha-Metim* is the resurrection of the dead. Those who believe in the resurrection of Messiah Yeshua believe that they do not have to wait until after the Messianic era to be resurrected. While the Song of Moses begins with dire plagues and consequences for disobedience to the Torah, the Song ends with the return to the Land and final redemption, and that reminder of resurrection:

> It is I who put to death and give life.
> I have wounded and it is I who heal.

> Rejoice, O nations, with His people;
> For He will avenge the blood of His servants,

> And will render vengeance on His adversaries,

34. The Garden of Eden, Paradise, Third Heaven, the lower garden.

35. *The Midrash Says*, p. 375

56

> And will atone for His land and His
> people. (Dt 32:39, 43)

The apostles speak of the resurrection into the Clouds of Glory, in which the Presence of Adonai guarded His people. There they will be with Yeshua, and there they will enjoy the benefits of the first resurrection during his reign. Because they believed the Song of Moses, and they lived by the Word of resurrection, including the Books of Moses, they have the proper garments of salvation and robes of righteousness to enter into the Kingdom. They can once again guard and serve in the Garden.

Those who sing the Song of Moses, the Fourth Song, can also sing the Song of the Lamb, the Tenth Song. Those whose lives sing with the performance of God's will with recognition that He and He alone is the Master of the heavenly and earthly regions, that He and He alone is to be feared, loved, and served... those children will sing the Song of the Lamb.

The Techiat Ha-metim According to John

Then I saw thrones, and they sat on them, and judgment was given to them. And I saw the souls of those who had been beheaded because of their testimony of Jesus and because of the word of God, and those who had not worshiped the beast or his image and had not received the mark on their forehead and on their hand; and they came to life and reigned with Christ for a thousand years. The rest of the dead did not come to life until the thousand years were completed. This is the first resurrection. Blessed and holy is the one who has a part in the first resurrection; over these the second death has no power, but they will be priests of God and of Christ and will reign with Him for a thousand years. When the thousand years are completed, Satan will be released from his prison, and will come out to deceive the nations which are in the four corners of the earth, Gog and Magog, to gather them together for the war; the number of them is like the sand of the seashore. And they came up on the broad plain of the earth and surrounded the camp of the saints and the beloved city, and fire came down from heaven and devoured them. And the devil who deceived them was thrown into the lake of fire and brimstone, where the beast and the false prophet are also; and they will be tormented day and night forever and ever. Then I saw a great white throne and Him who sat upon it, from whose presence earth and heaven fled away, and no place was found for them. And I saw the dead, the great and the small, standing before the throne, and books were opened; and another book was opened, which is the book of life; and the dead were judged from the things which were written in the books, according to their deeds. And the sea gave up the dead which were in it, and death and Hades gave up the dead which were in them; and they were judged, every one of them according to their deeds. Then death and Hades were thrown into the lake of fire. This is the second death, the lake of fire. And if anyone's name was not found written in the book of life, he was thrown into the lake of fire. (Re 20:4-15)

Psalm 92

A Psalm, a Song for the Sabbath Day

It is good to give thanks to the LORD
And to sing praises to Your name, O Most High;
To declare Your lovingkindness in the morning
And Your faithfulness by night,
With the ten-stringed lute and with the harp,
With resounding music upon the lyre.
For You, O LORD, have made me glad by what You
have done,
I will sing for joy at the works of Your hands.
How great are Your works, O LORD!
Your thoughts are very deep.
A senseless man has no knowledge,
Nor does a stupid man understand this:
That when the wicked sprouted up like grass
And all who did iniquity flourished,
It was only that they might be destroyed
forevermore.
But You, O LORD, are on high forever.
For, behold, Your enemies, O LORD,
For, behold, Your enemies will perish;
All who do iniquity will be scattered.
But You have exalted my horn like that of the wild
ox;
I have been anointed with fresh oil.
And my eye has looked exultantly upon my foes,
My ears hear of the evildoers who rise up against
me.
The righteous man will flourish like the palm tree,
He will grow like a cedar in Lebanon.
Planted in the house of the LORD,
They will flourish in the courts of our God.
They will still yield fruit in old age;
They shall be full of sap and very green,
To declare that the LORD is upright;
He is my rock, and there is no unrighteousness in
Him.

THE SONG OF MIRIAM

Beshalach "and sent"
Exodus 13:17-17:16
Judges 4:4-5:31
Psalm 66

Shabbat Shirah (Sabbath of Song) is the Shabbat when synagogues read the parasha *Beshalach*.[36] This *parasha* includes the Second Song, the Song at the Sea. These are the praises which were sung by the Israelites after the Egyptians had drowned in the Sea of Reeds.[37] In some synagogues, this song is chanted in a special cantillation. Since the parting of the sea is celebrated as a great miracle and the climactic episode to the exodus from Egypt, the Song at the Sea has become associated with thanksgiving and praise.

Jewish tradition teaches that there are only ten true songs in the history of the world. They are more than melodies; they are expressions of the harmony of creation and mark significant transitions in Israel's spiritual history.

The *Haftorah* portion of Beshalach also contains another one of these songs, the Song of Deborah (Judges 5:1-3). The Song of Deborah is the Sixth

36. Exodus 13:17-17:16

37. Mistakenly translated in English as Red Sea

61

Song. The sages teach that the Tenth and final song has not yet been sung; it is the Song of the coming of Messiah which will be sung at the end of days.[38]

It is Miriam and the Israelites women's echoing of the Song at the Sea that makes it so distinct. Their lyrics mirror Moses', and the distinct grammar of the song is a wondrous prophecy concerning the Divine Chariot that can only later be viewed more distinctly through the eyes of Ezekiel and Elisha.

> Miriam the prophetess, Aaron's sister, took the timbrel in her hand, and all the women went out after her with timbrels and with dancing. Miriam answered them, 'Sing to the LORD, for He is highly exalted; the horse and his rider He has hurled into the sea.' (Ex 15:20–21).

The song sounds poetic because there is a use of synecdoche, a lyrical technique in which the writer or singer will use the part to represent the whole. In this case, the singular "horse and rider" represent the many horses and riders of Pharaoh's chariots. In Hebrew, the driver of a chariot is not distinguished from the rider of the horse as it is in English. As an example, the chariot drivers in Zechariah are viewed as riders by John:

Rider (Revelation 6)
=
Chariot Driver (Zechariah 6)

Miriam, however, is a prophetess. Words are not random in Scripture, so the singular words may poetically refer to many chariots, or the singular words may allude to a specific horse and rider that was destroyed at the Sea. Miriam always appears

38. Is 26:1

62

in relation to water: the Nile, the Reed Sea, the Cushite,[39] and the loss of water to the camp in the wilderness.

The description in Numbers 20:1 of the death of Miriam is immediately followed by the episode of the Waters of Meribah:

> 'Miriam died there […] The community was without water' (vv. 1–2).

> The Rabbis learn from this juxtaposition that Miriam's death resulted in the dearth of water; they accredited to her the existence of the well that accompanied the Israelites on their wanderings in the wilderness and provided them with drinking water. (Rashi to Numbers 20)

The well, according to the Rabbis, was one of the things created on the eve of the Sabbath at twilight;[40] they depict it as a wondrous well that flowed from itself, like a rock full of holes.[41] The well is portrayed in the ruins of a mural in the Dura Europus synagogue that was destroyed in the third century CE. In the mural, Miriam's Well has streams of water issuing forth to each of the tents of the twelve tribes of Israel. Although there are only tiny hints to Miriam's role within the Israelite camp, Micah prophesied:

> Indeed, I brought you up from the land of Egypt and ransomed you from the house of slavery, and I sent before you Moses, Aaron and Miriam. (Micah 6:4)

The Midrash lists the well among the three gifts that were given to Israel by merit of their leaders:

> *The manna was given on account of Moses, the pillar of cloud, by merit of*

39. Although the apparent misspeak about Moses' Cushite wife has a literal application, the First Mention of Cush is a location within the Rivers of Eden in Genesis Two.

40. Avot 5:6

41. Sukkah 3:11

> Aaron, and the well, by merit of Miriam.
> The well that then reappeared by
> merit of Moses is the one mentioned
> in the song of the well (Num. 21). All
> three gifts—the well, the manna and
> the cloud—finally disappeared upon
> the death of Moses. *According to the
> aggadah, this well continues to issue
> within the Sea of Galilee (Jerusalem
> Talmud Kilayim 9:3, 32 [c]).*

The wilderness journey was a prophecy of a future
redemption. The three constant miracles were
associated with the leadership of Moses, Aaron, and
Miriam.

> Then the sons of Israel, the whole
> congregation, came to the wilderness
> of Zin in the first month [Nissan]; and
> the people stayed at Kadesh. Now
> Miriam died there and was buried
> there. (Nu 20:1)

The text implies that Miriam died in the month of
Passover, the month of Nissan. This explains the very
next verse: "There was no water for the congregation,
and they assembled themselves against Moses
and Aaron." The first statement is the cause of the
second. With a keen eye for what is and isn't in
the text, the ancient sages noticed that something
is missing. Because the Israelites are grieving over
the loss of Miriam, they are discouraged. They lash
out at Moses and Aaron. This was wrong, but the
missing something might explain *why* they lashed
out as well as why Moses' and Aaron's reactions
were excessive. It also explains why the Holy One's
accusation against the brothers is that they did not
sanctify His Name.

That missing something is a time of mourning for
Miriam. It was customary to have a family period of
mourning for a close relative, and it was customary

(and Biblical) to have a set period of mourning for a national leader.

Aaron knew to mourn for a leader in order to sanctify the Name. When his two sons, Nadab and Abihu were killed by a holy fired for inappropriately offering the incense offering in the Tabernacle, Aaron was not allowed to leave the Tabernacle because the anointing oil was upon him. These were more than Aaron's sons, though. These were national leaders, priests who would succeed their father Aaron. In his grief, Aaron does not eat the sin offering, which makes Moses angry. Aaron answers him:

> 'When things like these happened
> to me, if I had eaten a sin offering
> today, would it have been good in
> the sight of the LORD?' When Moses
> heard that, it seemed good in his
> sight. (Le 10:19-20)

Tithes and offerings should not be eaten in grief. Grief is an emotion that is intertwined with the realm of death. However, grieving for a departed loved one is also expected in Scripture. Since Aaron was unable to mourn properly for his sons, the whole nation of Israel stepped in to mourn for their brothers and leaders, Nadab and Abihu:

> But your kinsmen, *the whole house of*
> *Israel*, shall bewail the burning which
> the LORD has brought about.

Even a human who had been hanged as punishment had to be removed from the tree before sundown. The corpse had to be handled with respect for the one in Whose image the human being was made. [42] David was grateful to the men of Jabesh-gilead who recovered Saul's and Jonathan's mutilated bodies from the wall of Beth-shan at great risk to give the bones a proper burial.[43]

42. Dt 21:23

43. 1 Sa 31:11-13

Mourning is an important part of spiritual life, for it is a time when emotion is permitted to overflow its boundaries. The spirit, which functions based on "it is written," not "I feel," permits the heavy and powerful emotions to overflow usual boundaries. Even today, funeral motorcades defy the traffic rules and stop lights until they reach the cemetery. The other traffic pulls to the side of the road to honor the dead and those grieving them. In this period of emotional chaos, mourners are not rebuked for their questions, anger, or sorrow. The sages ask:

> **Where were the days of mourning for the leader Miriam?**

It's not that the Israelites or Miriam's brothers didn't know she was a significant leader. Generations later, the Prophet Micah reminds the Israelites: "... and I sent before you Moses, Aaron and Miriam." [44] The Israelites needed to mourn for such a significant spiritual loss in their leadership. Tradition says that it was because of her merit that the rock that followed them in the wilderness to provide water from its well. Most believers have "spiritual" moms and dads who have guided them in their faith, not just birth moms and dads. One grieves for the loss of spiritual leaders just as one does for a beloved member of the natural family. In grief, the question "Why?" usually comes up many times:

> The people thus contended with Moses and spoke, saying, "If only we had perished when our brothers perished before the Lord! Why then have you brought the Lord's assembly into this wilderness, for us and our beasts to die here? Why have you made us come up from Egypt, to bring us in to this wretched place? It is not a place of grain or figs or vines

44. Micah 6:4

or pomegranates, nor is there water
to drink..."

Without the ability to vent emotionally during a set
period of mourning for Miriam, they vent anyway
about the water, an essential provision that they
connected with the presence of this righteous
woman among them. Moses and Aaron appear
to take the Israelites' accusations much more
personally than Adonai:

> Then Moses and Aaron came in from
> the presence of the assembly to the
> doorway of the tent of meeting and
> fell on their faces. Then the glory of
> the Lord appeared to them; and the
> Lord spoke to Moses, saying, 'Take the
> rod; and you and your brother Aaron
> assemble the congregation and
> *speak to the rock* before their eyes,
> that it may yield its water. You shall
> thus bring forth water for them out
> of the rock and let the congregation
> and their beasts drink...'

The reader can discern an utter lack of anger on the
part of the Holy One. In fact, He simply gives the
instructions to re-start the well flowing from the Rock.
One can almost sense the compassion in the words:
"Let the congregation and their beasts drink." The
tone changes when Moses picks up the rod:

> So Moses took the rod from before
> the Lord, just as He had commanded
> him; and Moses and Aaron gathered
> the assembly before the rock. And he
> said to them, '*Listen now, you rebels*;
> shall *we* bring forth water for you out
> of this rock?'

Wow. Easy does it, brothers. Perhaps also still in a
state of grief over their beloved sister, Moses and

Aaron lash out at the complainers and call them rebels. In their anger, Moses and Aaron confuse themselves with the Holy One. They think that "we" can bring forth water.

> Then Moses lifted up his hand and *struck the rock twice with his rod*; and water came forth abundantly, and the congregation and their beasts drank.

> But the Lord said to Moses and Aaron, '*Because you have not believed Me, to treat Me as holy in the sight of the sons of Israel*, therefore you shall not bring this assembly into the land which I have given them." Those were the waters of Meribah, because the sons of Israel contended with the Lord, and *He proved Himself holy among them.*'

Once the reader understands the significance of Miriam's well, the crime and consequences make complete sense. There was something about Miriam and that rock-well that was so profoundly holy and prophetic that disrespecting it could shorten her brothers' journey to the Promised Land. The oversight was on two levels. First, it was in not setting days of mourning for a departed leader. They knew to do it, but they didn't. Imagine that when Aaron died, what Moses must have thought when he set the days of mourning, something he neglected with his sister who sang the Second Song:

> When all the congregation saw that Aaron had died, all the house of Israel wept for Aaron thirty days. (Ex 20:29)

Perhaps that is why the Israelites sang the Third Song, the song of Miriam's well in her memory. And then Moses himself was officially mourned for thirty days:

> Although Moses was one hundred
> and twenty years old when he died,
> his eye was not dim, nor his vigor
> abated. So the sons of Israel wept
> for Moses in the plains of Moab thirty
> days; then the days of weeping and
> mourning for Moses came to an end.
> (Dt 34:7-8)

Sometimes Scripture teaches by what it records, and
sometimes it teaches by what it doesn't. The Third
Song may hold the key:

> From there they continued to Beer,
> that is the well where the LORD said
> to Moses, 'Assemble the people, that
> I may give them water.' Then Israel
> sang this song:
>
> Spring up, O well! Sing to it!
> The well, which the leaders sank,
> Which the nobles of the people dug,
> With the scepter and with their staffs.
> (Nu 21:16-18)

A simple song. At first glance, not so spectacular.
Yet from these simple words of the Third Song,
Jewish tradition records its prophecy. The Israelites
associated the well with Miriam. Once Moses re-
started the well, it nevertheless retained her memory
among the people. Moses and Aaron were the
"nobles" of Israel who struck the Rock with their staffs.
When the Israelites were about to cross over the
Jordan, and they would no longer rely on Miriam's
well for water, tradition says that Moses took the
rock-well and sank it to the bottom of the Galilee,
or Kinneret.

Whether Moses literally did it or not is not the point
of the story. It teaches an expectation of Messiah.
What Moses desecrated with his staff, he immersed

until a future time. It demonstrated to Israel that when Messiah came, he would identify with the rockwell of Miriam and come with songs of deliverance. He was the Yeshuat Adonai, the Salvation of Adonai, who parted the Reed Sea for the Israelites, just as Miriam was salvation for her baby brother Moses, placing him among the reeds and watching over him. Just as Yeshua destroyed the horse and his rider, throwing them into the Abyss at the Reed Sea, so a future Messiah would overthrow the horse and rider of Abaddon, confining them to the Abyss forever. This may explain why Miriam echoed Moses' Song of the Sea. The Second Song will be fulfilled twice!

Likewise, the Third Song may be fulfilled three times. When Moses and Aaron struck the Rock, water gushed out of it. When Messiah Yeshua taught from the Galilee and sent forth his fisherman, the water of the Word gushed out of it. When Messiah returns, the living waters of Eden will once again gush out of it.

In his ministry, Yeshua identified himself with the

1. Bread (manna) from Heaven, or "Moses."
2. The Angel of the Presence in the cloud (by asserting the power to forgive sin), or "Aaron."

In his affirmation that he was the Bread of Heaven from the Garden above, Yeshua corrects Moses' and Aaron's mistake of identifying themselves as the ones who would bring forth water from the rock. Instead, it was the Father in Heaven. Their staffs were merely instruments: "Jesus then said to them, 'Truly, truly, I say to you, it is not Moses who has given you the bread out of heaven, but it is *My Father who gives you* the true bread out of heaven.'"[45] On more than one occasion, Yeshua even supernaturally multiplies physical bread, and there are baskets left over. On one occasion, Yeshua multiplies the bread in a "desolate place," just as the manna fell in the wilderness.[46]

45. Jn 6:32
46. Mk 8:4

Yeshua's ministry as Bread of Heaven confirmed the sign of Moses. The second sign was the sign of Aaron, the ministry of the Angel of the Presence in the cloud.[47]

For forty years in the wilderness, the Israelites were educated in holiness, acquiring Yeshua's garments, the holy commandments. They learned to obey the Father, which meant they had to obey the judgment of the Angel in the cloud, who had the Divine Name and voice within him.

> Behold, I am going to send an angel before you to guard you along the way and to bring you into the place which I have prepared. Be on your guard before him and *obey his voice; do not be rebellious toward him, for he will not pardon your transgression, since My Name is in him.* But if you truly *obey his voice* and do all that I say, then I will be an enemy to your enemies and an adversary to your adversaries.[48]

That Angel protected them on the journey and brought them to the Land of Israel, a place of resurrection, but the prerequisite was obedience. They may have been a people saved from Egypt, but it did not transform them immediately into a holy, obedient nation fit for a resurrection Garden. The transgressions still residing within them would make their residence in the Promised Land short. It was only Moses who achieved a glow of light radiating from his face in his intimacy with the voice and commandments.

The Angel in the Cloud had a special attribute and ability, the power to forgive sin. This was a power of judgment assigned to him by the Holy One. This power of forgiving or not forgiving sin was important,

47. The following section is reproduced from *50,000 Degrees and Cloudy: A Better Resurrection* by the author.

48. Ex 23:20-22

for the Angel was tasked with guiding and protecting Israel until they reached the Holy Land.

> The LORD said to Moses, 'Whoever has sinned against Me, I will blot him out of My book. But go now, lead the people where I told you. Behold, *My angel shall go before you*; nevertheless *in the day when I punish*, I will punish them for their sin.' Then the LORD smote the people, because of what they did with the calf which Aaron had made.[49]

The Angel was sent with judgment power. There were books in Heaven that recorded the deeds of each individual. The books were still open until "The Day" of punishment for sin. The Angel in the cloud played a role in leading Israel. He would not pardon for rebellious, and we might assume, un-repented sins. He could not, for he had to act according to the will of the Divine Name and power within him. If he had the power *not* to pardon rebellious sin, then the obverse should be true: he had the power to forgive a repentant sinner.

This delegated power to forgive or not forgive transgressions appears again in Messiah Yeshua:

> I have come *as Light* into the world, so that everyone who believes in Me will not remain in darkness. *If anyone hears My sayings and does not keep them, I do not judge him*; for I did not come to judge the world, but to save the world. *He who rejects Me and does not receive My sayings, has one who judges him; the word I spoke is what will judge him at the last day. For I did not speak on My own initiative, but the Father Himself who sent Me has given Me a commandment as*

49. Ex 32:33-35

to what to say and what to speak. I know that *His commandment is eternal life*; therefore, the things I speak, *I speak just as the Father has told Me.*[50]

Yeshua identifies himself with the Torah, the Father's instructions to His children Israel, for the "Torah is a Light, and the commandment is a Lamp." The Angel of the Presence had the authority of the Father in the wilderness to speak His Word, and the Angel's Presence was binding because the Name, and therefore the deeds, of the Father were in him. The Angel did not speak of his own initiative, but reflected exactly the living Word of the Father by which Israel was judged. Yeshua identifies himself according to this "cloud" pattern and reminds his listeners that the same Word will judge them in the last day.

> And they brought to Him a paralytic lying on a bed. Seeing their faith, Jesus said to the paralytic, 'Take courage, son; *your sins are forgiven.*' And some of the scribes said to themselves, *'This fellow blasphemes.'* And Jesus knowing their thoughts said, 'Why are you thinking evil in your hearts? Which is easier, to say, "'Your sins are forgiven,'" or to say, "'Get up, and walk'"?
>
> ...*But so that you may know that the Son of Man has authority on earth to forgive sins'*-then He said to the paralytic, 'Get up, pick up your bed and go home.' And he got up and went home. But when the crowds saw this, they were awestruck, and *glorified God, who had given such authority to men.*[51]

The crowd's reaction is significant. Yeshua was a

50. Jn 12:46–50

51. Mt 9:2-8

man, yet he had authority to forgive, so he was no ordinary human being. They were awestruck by this authority, which had been given to the Angel of the Holy One's Presence to lead Israel home. Yeshua came with the second sign, the royal throne authority of the Divine Name within the Angel of the Presence as a remembrance of Aaron, whose service was to direct Israel to the altar, offer, and eat their sin offerings. He was also a judge of *tzaraat*, conditions of ritual impurity that barred a person from entering the holier places of the Tabernacle. Through following the priest's teaching of the Word, a person could be healed.

This brings the reader back to Miriam's well. Yeshua did identify himself with Miriam's well, giving drink to the Israelites. Yeshua proclaimed at the water-drawing ceremony in the Temple at the feast of Sukkot:

> Now on the last day, the great day of the feast, Jesus stood and cried out, saying, 'If anyone is thirsty, let him come to Me and drink. He who believes in Me, as the Scripture said, "'From his innermost being will flow rivers of living water.'" But this He spoke of the Spirit, whom those who believed in Him were to receive; for the Spirit was not yet given, because Jesus was not yet glorified. (Jn 7:37-39)

Yeshua's attitude was much different than Moses' and Aaron's on the day of striving at the rock.
What a beautiful, holy sanctification of the Spiritual waters sent from above.

Miriam's Well was concealed in the Kinneret until the arrival of Messiah, just like the manna of Moses and the authority to heal and cleanse sin like Aaron. Yeshua loved the Galilee, ministering there first, calling disciples there first, walking on its waters, and disciplining the stormy waters. After his resurrection, he returns there to meet his disciples and cooks fish.

> Jesus said to them, 'Do not be afraid; go and take word to My brethren to leave for Galilee, and there they will see Me.' (Mt 28:10)

Yeshua assured his brothers that he had fulfilled the final sign, the sign of Miriam's rock-well. He was the Rock in the wilderness that gave drink to the tribes of Israel; he was the manna that surrounded them each morning; he was the Presence of the Holy One in their midst.

> For I do not want you to be unaware, brethren, that our fathers were all under the cloud and all passed through the sea; and all were baptized into Moses in the cloud and in the sea; and all ate the same spiritual food; and all drank the same spiritual drink, for they were drinking from a spiritual rock which followed them; and the rock was Christ. (1 Co 10:1-4)

Paul teaches the Corinthians this ancient Midrash about the cloud, the bread, and the water because it is so significant to why Yeshua came from the Galilee even though he was born in Bethlehem. If anyone is thirsty...

5

THE SONG OF THE LEVITES

Naso "lift up"
Numbers 4:21-7:89
Judges 13:2-25
Psalm 67
Ephesians 5:6-20

Ever feel like there's more going on in the Bible than you're grasping in English? That's a good thing, because it keeps readers curious. As long as a Bible student is curious, she's studying. As long as she's studying, she's learning. As long as she's learning, she is less threatened that there is so much left to learn. Spiritual life now is getting a leg up on an eternity of learning.

The Torah portion Naso has a pretty straightforward English translation of the call to the Levites for service in the Tabernacle (Mishkan), also called the Tent of Meeting:

> ...from thirty years and upward even to fifty years old, everyone who could enter to do the work of service and the work of carrying in the tent of meeting. (Nu 4:47)

מִבֶּן שְׁלֹשִׁים שָׁנָה וָמַעְלָה וְעַד בֶּן־חֲמִשִּׁים שָׁנָה כָּל־הַבָּא
לַעֲבֹד עֲבֹדַת עֲבֹדָה וַעֲבֹדַת מַשָּׂא בְּאֹהֶל מוֹעֵד:

A Levite served for 20 years "on" his burden and work, a significant hint to "service." The number 20 has a corresponding Hebrew letter, *kahf* כ. Many words are formed from the *kahf*, all having something to do with being a vessel, container, or covering for another thing. A kippah is a Jewish religious cap, an upside-down vessel for the head. Yom Kippur is a Day of Covering, or atonement. A spoon is a cupped utensil, a *kapit*. Picture the palm of your hand as being a "cup," and that's a great visual, which matches the cup-like shape of *kahf*. Wearing a kippah is like having a hand cupped upon one's head in prayer.

Numbers 4:47 is translated in the Artscroll version in such a way that it preserves the strange turn of phrase in Hebrew:

> ...everyone who comes to perform service of a service [*la-avod avodat*] **and** the work of carrying the Tent of Meeting.

Avad is the Hebrew root that means service or work. This root appears four times in this one little fragment of a verse.

The seeds of the whole Scripture are in the Torah, so one wonders, where is the establishment of the Levitical singers in the Tabernacle and Temple services? The great Jewish scholar Rashi says it is right here in the "work and service" text. There is a service that *accompanies* the service of assembling, servicing, dismantling, and carrying the Tent of Meeting. The *la-avod-avodat* is the song performed with cymbals and harps, a service done for another service: carrying and serving in the Tent.

There were singing men and women who returned from Babylon to Israel in the time of Ezra the Prophet:

> The whole assembly numbered 42,360, besides their male and female servants who numbered 7,337; and they had 200 singing men and women. (Ezra 2:64-65)

These singing men and women sang to accompany certain types of holy services, mourning, and especially to preserve events in Scripture:

> And Jeremiah lamented for Josiah: and all the singing men and the singing women spoke of Josiah in their lamentations to this day, and made them an ordinance in Israel: and, behold, they are written in the lamentations. (2 Ch 35:25)

Scripture was preserved in song. The Song of Creation begins in Genesis One. There is no confusion in the song. Creation is orderly, numbered (as the days in the Torah portion), and fruitful within all the boundaries sung to establish it. Likewise, the song of the Levites accompanied by harps and cymbals is established for erecting, carrying, setting up, and working within the Tent of Meeting.

The traditional Psalm is 67 for Naso. It fuses the song of strings, the Aaronic benediction, and the earth's "produce," its people. Those people will return to the Song of Creation in the Torah.

Israel's Tabernacle and Temple were to be "a house of prayer for all nations," a light and song in the darkness to return the earth back to its spoken and sung order. The song is the mystery of the Word, the spirit that moves those things which are spiritual to natural and which are natural to spiritual. Song bridges the gap. The salvation songs sung in the Tabernacle bring humankind back to its center, the fruitful Garden, through the resurrection of Yeshua, the Singer who surrounds Israel with songs of deliverance.

There is an anomaly in Naso's record of the gold ladles filled with incense, a doubled number "ten":

> Rabbi Shimon bar Yochai taught: *cahf asarah asarah* - 'Each incense bowl weighed ten sanctuary shekels.' - literally: each bowl ten ten. Why (the doubled words) "'ten ten?'" Once, to allude to the work of creation, and once to allude to the Torah. There are ten utterances in the creation of the world, and (corresponding to them) ten utterances in the Torah (the Ten Commandments).

Each of the twelve "ten-weight" ladles was gold (*zahav*), yet they were weighed by a ten-weight of the holy shekel, which is silver. So were the ladles silver or gold? Yes. Gold by substance, silver by weight.

Good Gold[52] was in the Garden, a symbol of Adam and Eve, who were "very good" creations. Silver is the Biblical symbol of redemption, *geulah*. Here is a picture of restoration of prayer in the Garden:

> When Moses arrived at the Tent of Meeting to speak with Him, he heard the voice communicating with him from atop (*me-al*) the Cover (*ha-caporet*) that was upon the Ark of the Testimony, from between the two Cheruvim, and He spoke to him." (Nu 7:89)

52. Ge 2   In the Tent of Meeting, songs of communication were re-opened between the two cherubim, who were

located at the entrance back to the Garden. The original incense was the prayer, direct conversations with the Creator.

---

cahf = incense ladle
cahporet = cover
al = how the Levites served,
literally "on top of" the burden and service

There was a "Tent of Meeting" for Adam and Eve in the Garden. Their incense was offered in Good Gold vessels that Elohim created for them:

> It is He who sits above the circle [*chug*] of the earth...Who stretches out the heavens like a curtain and spreads them out like a tent [*ohel*] to dwell in. (Is 40:22)

A *chug* is the same root word as *chag*, another word for *moedim*, the appointed times of Israel. The whole circle of the earth moves according to the schedule of Heaven. Even the golden menorah can represent the movement of the planets around the "sun" at its center, similar to an atom. Under this *Ohel Moed*, or Tent of Meeting, Adam and Eve could meet Elohim. The Ohel Moed in the wilderness re-creates this Creation Song, the voice of many waters from the Rivers of Eden.

When Good Gold, Adam and Eve, the appointed rulers of the Earth, introduced confusion into themselves, they fell into the natural sphere. They weren't "on" their song, their service, their work to guard the Garden and their relationship with the Creator. Two cherubim were put in place to guard the Garden so that they wouldn't live forever in a condition that made them abhorrent to Elohim. He would send a Redeemer, silver for Gold.

Every soul carries a burden, but the Israelite must have control OVER the work and burden. That means the *nefesh* (soul) must be under the control of the Spirit so that it will not betray its service and be shamed and naked. Song is a bridge between the spirit and soul. Song is the bridge between the Garden and the natural world below it. When the song bridges the spirit and soul, then the "yoke" of the Kingdom becomes light, balanced between spiritual realm above and the physical realm below. According to this perfect balance we were created.

Adam and Eve's sin was betrayed by their clothes... or lack of. One of the garments (*begedim*) that the high priest had to wear in the Tent of Meeting was the *me'il*,[53] a robe. Its root is:

> מעל mâ'al; to cover up; used only
> figuratively, to act covertly, i.e.
> treacherously: transgress, (commit,
> do a) trespass(-ing).

The priest's robe covers the transgression of the betrayal in the Garden, and it reminds believers not to betray their work of guarding and working ON their service, their song, their prayer:

> He counted them at the word of
> HASHEM, through Moses, every man
> OVER his work and OVER his burden...
> (Artscroll) [54]

עַל־פִּי יְהֹוָה פָּקַד אוֹתָם בְּיַד־מֹשֶׁה אִישׁ אִישׁ **עַל־עֲבֹדָתוֹ וְעַל־מַשָּׂאוֹ**
וּפְקֻדָיו אֲשֶׁר־צִוָּה יְהֹוָה אֶת־מֹשֶׁה :

עַל = "on" or "over"

Song is a way of bridging the gap of communication between the Israelite and the Holy One, and next between Israelite and Israelite, and then from Israelite to the nations. It calls humankind back to the Song

53. Strong's 4598
54. Nu 4:49

of Creation, before betrayal, a restoration of Good Gold through Silver Redemption. No shame. Song is a way of being "on the job" of spiritual service.

In Ephesians 5:6-20, Paul reminds the believers at Ephesus of this Torah portion, one that offers the possibility of a Nazirite vow[55] to limit natural wine and to increase spiritual wine:

> So then do not be foolish, but understand what the will of the Lord is. And do not get drunk with wine, for that is dissipation, but be filled with the Spirit, speaking to one another in psalms and hymns and spiritual songs, singing and making melody with your heart to the Lord; always giving thanks for all things in the name of our Lord Jesus Christ to God, even the Father... (17-20)

So let's get ON our spiritual service. Bang cymbals and strum harps, whatever the world will receive. Let's get to work singing the Word!

55. Nu 6:2-3

6

YESHUA, THE SINGING PREACHER

All Torah portions
All the Prophets
All the Psalms
All the Writings

Did Yeshua twitter? The answer may be surprising.
King David was known as The Sweet, Sweet Singer
of Israel. King David is the acknowledged shadow
of Messiah. While other Scriptural characters present
aspects of Messiah, the Messiah is the shoot of
Jesse[56] and the Son of David. The two are so alike
that in Jeremiah 30:9 the prophet calls Messiah
David: "But they shall serve the LORD their God and
David their king, whom I will raise up for them..."

When it comes to David, one might think that he
first came to the attention of Israel as their deliverer
when he killed Goliath. The obvious answer is his
courage in the face of adversity, but what about his
unparalleled musical talent that first brought him to
the attention of King Saul? From youth until old age,
David was a sweet singer of spiritual songs. His songs
could drive away oppressive evil spirits. Even David's
last words are recorded in a song:

Now these are the last words of David.   56. Is 11:1

David the son of Jesse declares,
The man who was raised on high declares,
The anointed of the God of Jacob,
And the sweet psalmist of Israel,
The Spirit of the LORD spoke by me,
And His word was on my tongue.
(2 Sa 23:1-2)

So the reader looks for clues about Messiah Yeshua that reflect the nature of King David, the Sweet Singer of Israel. Other than singing the Great Hallel of Psalm 136 after Passover, there is little in the Gospels that suggest that Yeshua was a psalmist or singer. Nevertheless, that surprise tweet is found in a closer study of the texts and First Century Jewish history.

The Nazarene

Yeshua was known as "The Nazarene." In the Aramaic New Testament, he is called *Yeshua HaNotzri*. The title was even nailed to the cross with him. The reader must ask, "Was this intended to denote his hometown or the actual *charge* for which he was sentenced to die? His followers were known as Nazarenes even after his death, resurrection, and ascension.

Blind Bartimaeus' reaction is interesting: "When he heard that it was Jesus the Nazarene, he began to cry out and say, 'Jesus, Son of David, have mercy on me!'"[57] Perhaps it was more than hearing that it was Yeshua from the town of Nazareth that caused such an enthusiastic reaction from Bartimaeus. His address to the "Son of David" is as significant as the actual meaning of "Nazarene."

If "Nazarene" was only a way of denoting Yeshua's hometown, then it is odd that even his followers were given the name. Although some may have come from near the little hamlet of Nazareth in the Galilee, there is no evidence Yeshua selected or received any disciples from his

57. Mk 10:47

86

hometown. In fact, his hometown folks were less than welcoming. They tried to push him over a cliff!

A respected Jewish rabbi and scholar who survived the Holocaust and later converted to Christianity was Israel Eugenio Golli. He was the chief rabbi of Rome. Working from his extensive knowledge of Biblical Hebrew, Aramaic, Greek, and Arabic, Rabbi Golli investigated the term "Nazarene" as it was used in the *Brit HaChadashah* (New Testament). After an exhaustive analysis, he concluded that the grammatical structure of the word in context as a place-name title was not a good fit for a word intended to describe both Yeshua and his disciples.

The Scripture that leads most to conclude that Yeshua was called a Nazarene because of his hometown is Matthew 2:23:

> Then after being warned by God in a dream, he left for the regions of Galilee, and came and lived in a city called Nazareth. This was to fulfill what was spoken through the prophets: 'He shall be called a Nazarene.'

The problem is that Nazareth is not mentioned in the Prophets, or even in the entire Tanakh! There is no direct quote that says the Messiah will be called a Nazarene. Rabbi Golli, however, investigated the Prophets thoroughly, and he concluded that they *do* say that the Messiah will be a Nazarene, but the difference is that he will be called The Branch, *netzar*,[58] in Isaiah 11:1.

The Notzri: The Branch

The root *natzar*[59] denotes the acts of...

> guarding, watching over, preserving, and observing

58. Strong's #H5342

59. Strong's #H5341

87

This definition of Nazarene is more apropos to the person of Yeshua than merely a hometown. The verb natzar is often used in the context of keeping the Torah covenant and preserving life, sometimes by hiding. The most overwhelming use of natzar, however, is in relation to keeping the testimonies, commandments, and statutes of the Torah.

This context of *natzar* is consistent with Yeshua's assertion that he had not come to abolish the Torah or Prophets in Matthew Five, but to fulfill them and bring them to their fullest meaning:

> Whoever then annuls one of the least of these commandments, and teaches others to do the same, shall be called least in the kingdom of heaven; but WHOEVER KEEPS AND TEACHES THEM, he shall be called great in the kingdom of heaven. (Mt 5:19)

Here in **bold** print are only a few examples of *natzar* in the songs of the Sweet Singer and other psalmists:

> You are my hiding place; You **preserve me** from trouble; You surround me with songs of deliverance. Selah. (Psalm 32:7)

> For the choir director. A Psalm of David. Hear my voice, O God, in my complaint; **preserve my life** from dread of the enemy. (Psalm 64:1)

> That they should put their confidence in God and not forget the works of God, but **keep His commandments**. (Psalm 78:7)

> So that they might keep His statutes and **observe** His laws, Praise the

LORD! (Psalm 105:45)

How blessed are those who **observe** His testimonies, who seek Him with all their heart. (Psalm 119:2)

Take away reproach and contempt from me, for I **observe** Your testimonies. (Psalm 119:22)

Teach me, O LORD, the way of Your statutes, and I shall **observe** it to the end.

Give me understanding, that I may **observe** Your law and keep it with all my heart. (Psalm 119:34)

This has become mine, that I **observe** Your precepts. (Psalm 119:56)

The arrogant have forged a lie against me; with all my heart I will **observe** Your precepts. (Psalm 119:69)

I understand more than the aged, because I have **observed** Your precepts. (Psalm 119:100)

Depart from me, evildoers, that I may **observe** the commandments of my God. (Psalm 119:115)

Your testimonies are wonderful; therefore, my soul **observes** them. (Psalm 119:129)

All the preceding examples of natzar inextricably link the identity of the Messiah, the Netzar, to the Word of God, especially the covenant of the Torah.

Jews of the First Century were quite comfortable

with wordplay, so the essential meaning of Nazarene may have included Yeshua's hometown only as a secondary meaning. The primary meaning directly links Yeshua to the Sweet Singer of Israel and the Prophets' assertion that The Branch will be one whose vitality originates in keeping the covenant of the Father.

Twittering Rabbis and Preachers

Yeshua the Nazarene (Aramaic: *Yeshua HaNotzri*) may also be understood as Yeshua the Singing Preacher. His disciples were also recognized as singing proclaimers of the Gospel. Even Paul, though not one of the disciples, practices the rabbinic and Jewish custom of singing prayers:

> What is the outcome then? I will pray with the spirit and I will pray with the mind also; I will sing with the spirit and I will sing with the mind also. (1 Co 14:15)

The Aramaic root of Nazarene is natzar, and the noun form natzora means "preacher." Aramaic was the lingua franca of the Galilee. In Aramaic, "'Nazarene' holds also the concept of preacher and teacher."[60] In Syriac, netzar means "to sing, to trill, to twitter," or "to sing, to declaim a poem." In the context of Jeremiah 31:6-7, the word notzrim means" singers, heralds."[61]

Applying the Aramaic meaning of Nazarene, Yeshua and his disciples were known as "the preachers, the declaimers."[62] Yeshua was charged before Pilate not because he was from Nazareth, but because he preached in a way that moved people mightily! He was Yeshua the Nazarene, Yeshua the Preacher.

60. Golli, p. 47

61. ibid, p. 41

62. ibid, p. 46

Even today, rabbis who are teaching will move into and out of a singsong for emphasis. This is an ancient custom. Preaching is simultaneously an act of singing, as is prayer or reading from the Scriptures. Can't you just hear Yeshua singing the Beatitudes to the multitude? Golli acknowledges that there is no tacit mention of Yeshua or his disciples singing in declamation of the Gospel, yet he cautions:

> If in the Gospel there is no mention of declamation simply because this form of exposition was no novelty to those accustomed to hear the rendering of the sacred texts in song, we should not exclude the fact that Jesus and His disciples made use of declamation too.[63]

In fact, Golli points out that rabbinical literature from that period of history cautions one who is translating from the actual Scriptures into Aramaic not to sing his translation song as loudly as the biblical text so as not to obscure the significance of the actual Hebrew text.[64]

Song was very much a part of the culture of Israel. According to Philo, the recitation that accompanied the presentation of a basket of fruit at Sukkot was in the form of a song.[65] Tractate Megillah 32a emphasizes the importance of reading Scripture as a song or modulation. Rabbi Akiva recommended singing one)s daily study of Scripture: «Zemer bekol yom, zemer bekol yom," or "A song each day, a song each day." The Bible was studied by singing a passage of it.

The scribes had introduced a *cantilena* (signs like musical notes) to aid reading and memorizing Scripture, and this eventually evolved into the existing system of *negginot*, or musical accents. Golli reports that Yemenite Jews, even adults, were quite unable to quote Scripture without singing it because that is how they learned it![66] There are special melodies for the Torah, Prophets, and Writings. The reading of a psalm is really the reading of a song as originally intended.

Yeshua's Harp: The Galilee

63. ibid, p. 52

64. ibid, p. 53

65. ibid, p. 43

The twittering Natzar may be broken into a Hebrew onomatopoeia, *tzor*. Onomatopoiea is a literary device in which words sound like their meaning. English examples might be woof, bang, zoom, tweet, crack, etc. *Tzor* in Hebrew mimics the sound of a cricket (*tzratzar*). This is similar to the ancient preachers who sang a portion of Scripture and then explained it in their sermons with melody.[67] Psalm 48:4 describes the act of teaching to the accompaniment of a harp.

Nazareth in the First Century was no more than a village. It was, however, located near the Kinneret (Lake of Galilee). The lake is called the Kinneret because its shape resembles a harp, the ancient instrument of King David, who played a *kinor*. [68] Yeshua's hometown was near the great harp of Israel, and he was its great preacher.

Although Nazareth (*Netzaret*) was considered a linguistic connection to Yeshua, the primary connection between Yeshua's actual work on earth and the Hebrew and Aramaic languages is the designation of Preacher. The risen Yeshua walked the Emmaus road listening patiently as his own disciples unwittingly also fulfill the roles of Proclaimer and Nazarene:

> And He said to them, 'What things?'
> And they said to Him, 'The things about Jesus the Nazarene, who was a prophet mighty in deed and word in the sight of God and all the people.'
> (Lk 24:19)

Even Paul in Chapter Fifteen of his Letter to the Romans emphasizes the song of praise that Gentiles can sing with Israel because of Yeshua's fulfillment of Isaiah's prophecy and his proclamation. In view of such rich history, to carry on a worship service of prayer and Scripture reading without song would be to omit the pattern of our Messiah

66. ibid, p. 43
67. ibid, p. 42
68. Strong's #H3658

Yeshua and his disciples. Prayers and Scripture readings become spiritual songs in addition to words of understanding. These songs aid comprehension and recall, and they invite the Spirit to move over the harpstrings of the listeners' hearts. What a beautiful heritage of the synagogue Yeshua passes on to successive generations who hear and proclaim him.

Here are Yeshua's final words to his disciples:

> And Jesus came up and spoke [G2980] to them, saying, 'All authority has been given to Me in heaven and on earth. Go therefore and make disciples of all the nations, baptizing them in the name of the Father and the Son and the Holy Spirit, teaching them to observe all that I commanded you; and lo, I am with you always, even to the end of the age.' (Mt 28:18-20)

The Greek word *laleo* (G2980) is translated as "spoke." It is a prolonged form of an otherwise obsolete verb that has several translations, among them "to preach. " Thayer's Greek Lexicon notes that the verb applies not only to human beings, but to the sounds of animals, most particularly birds or locusts, a close and kosher relative of the cricket (*tzratzar*), whose song is compared to the preaching of the ancient prophets.

Compare Yeshua the Nazarene's last song to his disciples to David's last words of song. The observance and proclamation of the commandments is what ties The Nazarene to The Branch. The Branch from the Root of Jesse is indeed the reality of the anointed King David, the Sweet Singer of Israel.

The early preaching of the Nazarenes was a loud, musical, and Spirit-filled proclamation of the Good Tidings of great joy. The loud proclamation of Yeshua at Sukkot in the Temple heralded an era of inspired teaching and preaching, for the Son of David was singing songs of deliverance.

> You are my hiding place; You
> preserve me from trouble;
> You surround me with songs of
> deliverance. Selah.
> I will instruct you and teach you in the
> way which you should go.
> (Ps 32:7-8)

Let the earth in these troubled times once again be awestruck at the Nazarenes who proclaim spiritual songs of deliverance like their rabbi, teacher, preacher, prophet, evangelist, and Messiah,

7

SONGS OF DELIVERANCE: THE SECRET TUNE OF THE SHALSHELET:

Tzav "Command!"
Leviticus 6:8-8:36
Jeremiah 7:21-8:3; 9:22-23
Psalm 107
Mark 9:17-27

Tzav is the imperative verb form from which the noun *mitzvah*, or commandment, is formed. Tzav! is not just to command someone to do something, but do it quickly! The listener feels the forward motion in the verb itself, short and to the point. The mitzvah is the commandment to be done quickly, in a hurry, such as eating the Pesach lamb. "Move it!" says the Holy One to Israel concerning the anointing of the Mishkan for service.

This parasha so logically and beautifully carries along the previous week's parasha, which begins with the verb of calling and endearment, "Vayikra." Call gently to the Israelites. From this intimate pause and contemplation of Vayikra, Israel springs into action with Tzav, the commandments of the Mishkan.

What's the difference in the content of the two

portions? After all, Tzav is essentially only a recap of previous ones. It provides a transition from the first parasha in the Book of Leviticus, called Vayikra. An Israelite contemplates and prepares to receive the holy message in Vayikra, and then the message is spoken with all the power and glory of the Divine Presence in Tzav.

The prophets speak of the tongues of angels, myriads of heavenly beings who call (*vayikra*) to one another and then say, "Holy, Holy, Holy."[69] The Torah portion named Vayikra and the book (Leviticus) are the same word as that used to describe how the angels "call" to one another. It is in perfect unity and love that the angels fulfill their roles, without jealousy. It is significant that Moses anoints Aaron in this portion as the Cohen HaGadol, or High Priest. As with his "pause" at Sinai of six days before he ascends the mountain, so Moses serves in the Mishkan for six days before he passes the service to Aaron for the role of High Priest to service it with the accompanying offerings.

One might wonder why Moses was told to perform this service with the urgency of Tzav! There are many related Hebrew words like vayikra, gentler, more endearing. He might simply say (*omer*) or speak (*daber*). It reminds me of the days when I learned and taught self-defense. The instructor gives the class or team a command to execute, which is then followed by the imperative, "Do it now!" This process assumes the class already knows what to do, and they will immediately spring into action. They know what and they know how. They've already been called, spoken to, and the information has been said. Now it is time to tzav. Do it now! This is true of this Torah portion. The Israelites recognize the commandments that have been detailed previously. When Moses or the people hear "Tzav!", they spring immediately into action to obey from their previous training.

69. Is 6:3

This is consistent with the Biblical pattern of doing before understanding. At Sinai, the Israelite said, "We will do and we will hear."[70] By doing first, they will come to understand, or hear. Moses has explained how to do things, giving detailed instructions. Now it is time to do them. "Hearing" them will come later, which means they will understand why later. They will learn the deeper meanings as they develop a life of obedience. Commandments are layered that way. The more a believer does the commandments, the more spiritual sense they make, and the less rational sense one craves in order to obey them.

It is at this point that Moses is told to "Do it now!" There may be a message embedded in Moses' being told to hurry up and do it without thinking about it too long. Moses forfeited the High Priesthood, as well as his descendants' priesthood, when he argued with the burning bush, not believing he was capable of all the Holy One was tasking him to do. The Divine answer is something like, "Fine. Then I'll put your brother ahead of you, and he'll speak for you." In essence, this is what the Cohen HaGadol does; he speaks for the nation he serves, bearing the people on his shoulders and heart.

Because Moses hesitated and argued at the burning bush, his sons would not be included in the priesthood to serve. They would be numbered among the Levites, yet not appointed as priests. The commandments of Adonai are to be performed quickly and with joy. Was this a case where Moses was tempted to hesitate or lack joy? Not for himself, but for his sons, whom he'd excluded from priesthood by his ambivalence about serving Israel in the Holy One's great song of deliverance from Egypt. Part of him wanted to serve, but the other part was afraid and delayed. Like an ambidextrous person can use right or left hands equally well, a person who is ambivalent hesitates between two opinions, delaying his immediate obedience.

70. Ex 24:7

Songs of Ambivalence

The Torah is a song. In the course of each year, the entire song of the Torah is sung in synagogues around the world. It is another understanding of what it means to sing the "Song of Moses." The weekly portions become songs detailing the stories, procedures, and above all, prophecies of Israel's deliverance from death, the grave, and hell. When the Torah was finally recorded with cantillation marks like the score to a song, nuances of the text that found their way into the ears of those who heard the Torah song were preserved. Even for those experiencing advanced dementia, song clings tightly in the recesses of the mind and heart, the places where the Shema commands love and remembrance for Adonai, the song-giver of deliverance.

In Leviticus 8:23 reads concerning Aaron's ordination service for the priesthood:

> And he slaughtered it; and Moshe took of its blood, and put it on the tip of Aharon's right ear, and on the thumb of his right hand, and on the toe of his right foot. (Artscroll)

The first word of the verse, va-yishchat [and slaughtered] has a cantillation mark called the shalshelet. It is the squiggly line over the fourth letter from the right. It requires the Torah singer to repeat the succession of notes three times on one syllable.[71] For those who have never heard it, imagine a singer warming up his or her voice before a performance, moving up and down the musical scales: va-yishcha-ah-ah-AH-ah-ah-ah-ah-AH-ah-ah-ah-ah-ah-AH-ah-ah-at.

71. You can hear it here: http://bible.ort.org/webmedia/t3/0823.mp3

The shalshelet is a rare cantillation mark. It appears only three times prior to Tzav:

> But Lot lingered [va-yitmahmah]; and the men laid hold of his hand, and of his wife's hand, and of the hand of his two daughters, for God's mercy was upon him. And they brought him forth, and set him outside the city. (Ge 19:16)

The verse above is a "first mention" or use, of the shalshelet, which means it sets a theme or concept that the rest of its uses will follow, each explaining something about the other context. In this first mention, the shalshelet is a method of drawing the reader into Lot's story and heightening the tension the reader feels at Lot's ambivalence about leaving Sodom. The word for "Lot lingered" is sustained incredibly long in the last syllable, three loops of the same series of notes, which is difficult for the average reader to reproduce in the song.

Like Lot's lingering thinking, wanting to understand where he's going and thinking about what he's leaving behind before obeying the angel, the Torah cantor draws out the lingering word. The word is spooled out like taffy in the hands of an expert, dangling the listener over the fires of hell before singing the message of Lot's family's deliverance. Lot lingered when he knew what to do and how to do it. He lingered even when he had been Divinely ordained for mercy in destruction.

To ask "what" in Hebrew, one says, "Mah?" Say va-yitmahmah aloud, and it sounds as if Lot is saying in Hebrew, "What? What?" and prolonging it, like "Whaaaaaaaaaaaaat?" All believers must eventually answer the question of why they delay to do the right thing when that is the very source of deliverance and Divine mercy.

In the next mention, Abraham's servant prays concerning a wife for Isaac, using the shalshelet with "And he said...":

> And he said: 'Almighty God, the God of my master Avraham, please send me good fortune this day, and show kindness to my master Avraham.' (Ge 24:12)

Why was the servant ambivalent about what he prayed? Perhaps he knew that at one time, Abraham intended to bequeath his fortune to him. Instead, by Divine intervention, Abraham and Sarah were given a son to inherit from them. This is a great object lesson in the song of the Torah. Abraham had both worldly wealth and spiritual wealth. Now that the worldly wealth would pass to Isaac, the servant may have felt disinherited, separated from the relationship he had with Abraham. Nevertheless, in spite of his feelings, he prayed for the best outcome for Abraham and Isaac: a Godly wife.

While he and his descendants may not have received Abraham's worldly fortune, by praying through his ambivalence, the faithful servant could inherit Abraham's spiritual fortune of mercy and deliverance, just like all the families of the earth. The link to the shalshelet seems vague in this example, but perhaps it very closely resembles Moses' situation, a potential hesitation to act because of his sons' disinheritance from the priesthood. The physical, however, is finite, only reflecting the infinity of Heavenly service. Those servants gifted with a few things who serve gladly and who immediately invest those gifts in obedience are rewarded with riches still unseen by the human eye.

"We will do and we will hear [see, understand]" is a most profound prophetic statement of faith. It means that Israel will do the commandments according to their instructions. Yes, believers will experience levels of understanding in this life, but only in the Clouds of Glory will they truly begin to see and understand the point of the commandments. Abraham's servant experiences ambivalence in his mission, yet he prays through it. Sometimes, before the heart rejoices in the commandment, it must obey the commandment.

The healing of the deaf-mute in Mark Nine illustrates this. It is believed that at Sinai, there was a mass healing of all the sick in Israel. One tradition says that at first, the sound of the commandments caused the Israelites to die, then they would immediately be resurrected, similar to Paul's letter concerning the resurrection in the "twinkling of an eye."[72] The Israelites could not bear this repeated resurrection, and they begged Moses: "Speak to us yourself and we will listen; but do not have God speak to us, or we will die!"[73]

All stood at the foot of the mountain, so there were no lame. All saw the sounds, so there were no blind. Among the healings were the deaf and mute, for the entire nation said, "We will do and we will hear." When Messiah came, that would be a sign that he could deliver:

> Then one of the crowd answered and said, 'Teacher, I brought You my son, who has a mute spirit. And wherever it seizes him, it throws him down; he foams at the mouth, gnashes his teeth, and becomes rigid. So I spoke to Your disciples, that they should cast it out, but they could not.'
>
> He answered him and said, 'O faithless generation, how long shall I be with you? How long shall I bear with you? Bring him to Me.' Then they brought him to Him. And when he saw Him, immediately the spirit convulsed him, and he fell on the ground and

72. 1 Co 15:52

73. Ex 20:19

wallowed, foaming at the mouth. So
He asked his father, 'How long has
this been happening to him?' And
he said, 'From childhood. And often
he has thrown him both into the fire
and into the water to destroy him.
But if You can do anything, have
compassion on us and help us.'

Jesus said to him, 'If you can believe,
all things are possible to him who
believes.'

Immediately the father of the child
cried out and said with tears, 'Lord, I
believe; help my unbelief!'

When Jesus saw that the people
came running together, He rebuked
the unclean spirit, saying to it, 'Deaf
and dumb spirit, I command you,
come out of him and enter him
no more!' Then the spirit cried out,
convulsed him greatly, and came out
of him. And he became as one dead,
so that many said, 'He is dead.' But
Jesus took him by the hand and lifted
him up, and he arose. (Mk 9:17-27)

If the New Testament were written with cantillation
marks, it is not hard to imagine that the father's word
"believe" would have been sung with a shalshelet.
He wants to believe that Yeshua can heal, but his
experience is rooted in the physical reality of a deaf,
mute, and demon-possessed son. For the love of
his son, the father says he believes even when the
physical world is at war with his spirit, which has faith in
the Word of Yeshua. He says, "Forgive my unbelief."
Forgive my ambivalence. Both physical healing and
a type of resurrection followed for the family. Like
Lot, there was mercy on this family. Deliverance. In
the case of Abraham's servant, his prayer is likewise

answered when he prays on behalf of someone else, even when he struggles with ambivalence.

"Forgive my unbelief." Unbelief is usually accompanied by a lack of joy. It will be impossible not to believe joyfully at Sukkot, when one finally dwells in shelters and rewards of eternity for faith at Passover and Shavuot. In the meantime, the believing and unbelieving father and Abraham's servant teach all believers to pray and move forward at the command, even asking forgiveness for one's Lot-lingering doubts.

The third example in Genesis illustrates even more the struggle of unbelief in the soul, which is appetites, desires, emotion, and intellect, against the spirit, which comes from the Father above. There is a wrestling for control, seen when Joseph is tempted by Potiphar's wife:

> But Yosef refused, and said to his master's wife: 'Behold, my master, having me, knows not what is in the house, and he has put all that he has into my hand.' (Ge 39:8)

Joseph acknowledges that he's received great responsibility in the house of the Priest of On, just as Moses received great responsibility serving God's House. What Moses did not receive was the perpetual priesthood, which was given to Aaron. Joseph's soul is surely tempted as any young man would be, yet he acknowledges that physical responsibilities and gifts given to him by an earthly priest pale in comparison to the responsibility to the One who created the priest! His refusal, however, is marked by the shalshelet, the power of sexual desire and sin warring against the commandments he learned from his father Israel.

As disciples of Yeshua, believers cannot deny that sometimes they are ambivalent about the commandments. It is one thing to read them in the company of other believers, but quite another to practice them when tempted with physical gratification now, luxury now, comfort now, social standing now, safety now. The Song of the Torah assures its readers that the Father knows they will have times of ambivalence in applying His Word. The disciple will read it, and his spirit agrees, "We will do and we will hear!" The next day at work, or the family reunion, or with friends, that swift agreement with the Word in practice may be more hesitant.

Father, forgive our unbelief, but we DO believe! Your Torah Song of Deliverance and our faith in Yeshua's mercy delivers the weekly healing and resurrection we need to keep Your commandments and testimony until the end.

So was Moses jealous of his brother Aaron or those who prophesied in the camp? No! In Numbers 11:29, Moses says he wishes the whole nation were prophets. When Aaron led the people to the Golden Calf, Moses intercedes for his brother. Moses was not territorial or jealous. It could not be for himself that Moses hesitated to slaughter the animal of the consecration blood for Aaron and his sons.

Perhaps, like every believer, Moses considered his descendants and what he'd forfeited in his reluctance to lead at the burning bush. Nevertheless, he consecrated and anointed his brothers and nephews for the priesthood. In his temptation to linger over the slaughter, Moses remembers Tzav! Do it now, Moses. You'll understand later. In their own roles, your sons will prosper, never acquiring the bad reputations of rebels like your cousin Korach. Like you, they will be humble and serve. They won't be burned up for offering strange fire like Aaron's sons Nadab and Abihu, a 50% attrition rate! Your sons, like you, will provide the balance between zeal and humility.

If you've made mistakes of ambivalence in the past...if you've waited too long to believe in the mercy and deliverance of the Word...it will be normal to think about what you may have forfeited either for yourself or your children. Time lost. Opportunities wasted. It's okay. It's human. And you're in pretty good company: Moses, Abraham's servant, Joseph.

As the old Pentecostal saying goes, "Pray through" in those moments of hesitation when you are rooted in the limitations of your physical reality. Physical reality makes war with the spiritual heart that loves the commandments and the Commander of those commandments, so sing a song of deliverance. Draw it out until ambivalence departs. Sing that song louder and longer than your ambivalence, and you will know the compassion of the Father.

Go ahead. Belt it out.

Yeshu-ah-ah-ah--ah-AH-ah-ah-ah-ah-AH-ah-ah-ah-AH-ah-ah-ah-ah.

144,000 HARPS

Behar "On the Mountain"
Leviticus 25:1-26:2
Jeremiah 32:6-27
Psalm 112
Revelation 14:1-5

The Israelite year of agricultural and commercial release each seventh year leads to a Yovel, or Jubilee. It is a return, "each man to his family." We usually read about the Yovel as a physical return to the physical Land of Israel according to tribal affiliation. The Word, however, is both physical and spiritual.[74] If there is a natural goal of return to the family home and holdings every fifty years, then there is also a spiritual goal in returning to the physical Land.

Israel is the Resurrection Land, for the Garden of Eden hovers hidden just above it.[75] The Yovel becomes another way of illustrating how a believer is "gathered to his people." Instead of being gathered to the bones of an ancestral grave, the person is gathered to a living, producing, Land in a year when the produce is not *humanly* grown. It is food that the Holy One causes to grow, not as a result of plowing, planting, pruning, or cultivating. A year

74. Ro 7:14

75. See BEKY Book *50,000 Degrees and Cloudy: A Better Resurrection* by the author.

in Hebrew is *shanah*, which can mean more than just a year of time. It means a change, a transformation. The Land of Israel transforms naturally when Israel transforms spiritually.

The way the food grows in the Yovel year is similar to the description of the gourd that grew up over Jonah in his little hut after he prophesied to Nineveh. Jonah was upset that Nineveh was not destroyed, perhaps thinking they'd want to kill him as a false prophet. Nineveh had repented though, in sackcloth. Even the animals fasted and wore sackcloth![76] Adonai reminded Jonah that he had not planted the vine that shaded him, but the Creator. It was like a Yovel vine, and Jonah needed only to be obedient and rest, and then repentance and salvation would grow.

Jonah is also reminded that the Creator cares deeply for His human creations, but He cares, too, for the great number of animals that would be destroyed if he destroyed the Ninevites. All creation is groaning for the restoration of Israel and the restoration of their home in the Garden. Creation groans for plants grown a different way, a Heavenly way, through obedience.

The Garden's residents eat spiritual-natural food, returning the tribes to Eden, a spiritual-natural place that must be worked and guarded for a period of six years, then rested. When the seven *shmittah* years[77] were counted and completed, then the fiftieth year, the Yovel of free return, occurred. Apart from this process, Eden disappears from sight because humans "sell out" their faith in return and resurrection. You sell out, you move out. This is what happened to Adam and Eve in the Garden. This was the Creator's warning to Jonah who, after three days and three nights in a fish, resurrection, a smashingly successful evangelistic mission among the Gentiles, still was not "sold" on resurrection for the Ninevites.

76. Jonah 3:7-8

77. *Shmittah* years are years of rest every seventh year. After seven cycles of shmittah is the Yovel.

Even a "slave," whether pierced or not, must return to his ancestral property. This is not a slave in our Western understanding of a human as property. This type of "slave" either sold himself to work for unpaid debts (better), or the court sold him to work for unpaid debts or thefts for which he could not pay restitution (not as better). These Hebrew indentured servants had to be treated respectfully and on a level with the "master's" privileges in terms of comfort. In modern terms, if you contracted to work for a company for six years to pay off your unpaid debt, then your office and meal plan would have to be just as posh as the supervisor's. No wonder it fell out of fashion by the First Century.

On the cross at Golgotha, a thief was paying his debt the Roman way. The Hebrew way would have been to indenture him to work for someone until he repaid the restitution for his thefts. Yeshua forgave the thief of a much greater debt, and he assured the thief that he would return to his homeland "this day." There would be a transformation, a change, a return home.

In order to find the song of the Jubilee year, a re-reading of the text will identify the hints. Those hints can then lead us to the 144,000 harps of Yovel return.

> The LORD then spoke to Moses at Mount Sinai, saying, 'Speak to the sons of Israel and say to them, "'When you come into the land which I shall give you, then the land shall have a sabbath to the LORD. Six years you shall sow your field, and six years you shall prune your vineyard and gather in its crop, but during the seventh year the land shall have a sabbath rest, a sabbath to the LORD; you shall not sow your field nor prune your vineyard. Your harvest's aftergrowth you shall not

reap, and your grapes of untrimmed vines you shall not gather; the land shall have a sabbatical year. All of you shall have the sabbath products of the land for food; yourself, and your male and female slaves, and your hired man and your foreign resident, those who live as aliens with you. Even your cattle and the animals that are in your land shall have all its crops to eat.

You are also to count off seven sabbaths of years for yourself, seven times seven years, so that you have the time of the seven sabbaths of years, namely, forty-nine years. You shall then sound a ram's horn abroad on the tenth day of the seventh month; on the day of atonement you shall sound a horn all through your land. You shall thus consecrate the fiftieth year and proclaim a release through the land to all its inhabitants. It shall be a jubilee for you, and each of you shall return to his own property, and each of you shall return to his family. You shall have the fiftieth year as a jubilee; you shall not sow, nor reap its aftergrowth, nor gather in from its untrimmed vines. For it is a jubilee; it shall be holy to you. You shall eat its crops out of the field. On this year of jubilee each of you shall return to his own property.'" (Le 25:1-13)

Here is the important equivalency: do not sow your field or prune your vineyard. The reader thus derives:

> Sow your field ≈ prune your vinyeard

There is an example of a contranym in the Hebrew word for "prune." A contranym is its own opposite, such as "cleave" in English. The Hebrew contranym in the verse is from the root *zamar*:

> zâmar; to trim a vin: prune, to be pruned. #H559
> Lo *tizmor* = "you will not prune"

Zamar is to trim something, often something to be burned, like a thorn, or burned by fire, cut off, removed. It also means to plant in a vineyard as one sows a field. The Jewish scholar Rashi points out the slightly different contexts in verses 3 and 4:

> Six years you shall sow your field, and six years you shall prune [actively propagate] your vineyard and gather in its crop, but during the seventh year the land shall have a sabbath rest, a sabbath to the LORD; you shall not sow your field nor prune your vineyard.

There is a linguistic connection made by the root zamar, one of the Words that holds Creation together. Pruning is selectively choosing that which will yield to the gathering of fruit, and removing that which will not yield good fruit. That which is pruned away is for burning. The link is the word zamar, which in Hebrew is the playing and singing psalms of praise to the Holy One of Israel.

According to Jewish tradition, David was taught certain psalms when he hung up his harp at night. The wind would move through the strings and teach him the song. Psalms link two realms, supernatural and natural. Inspired combinations from the many waters above and the natural strings and human voices from below freely passed back and forth in the psalmists' night seasons. Sincerely played and prayed Psalms are unrestricted access to the Heavenlies, returning a person to his/her ancestral land, the Lower Garden of Israel.

> זָמַר zâmar; a primitive root (perhaps identical with H2168 through the idea of striking with the fingers); properly, to touch the strings or parts of a musical instrument, i.e. play upon it; to make music, accompanied by the voice; hence to celebrate in song and music: give praise, sing forth praises, psalms. **To pluck over and over.**

Like a vineyard worker who repetitively prunes a vine according to his vision of what he wants the vine to produce, a musician "prunes" a song from the many possibilities offered by every note and the instrument's strings.

> Then I looked, and behold, the Lamb was standing on Mount Zion, and with Him one hundred and forty-four thousand, having His name and the name of His Father written on their foreheads. And I heard a voice from heaven, like the sound of many waters and like the sound of loud thunder, *and the voice which I heard was like the sound of harpists playing on their harps.*
>
> *And they sang a new song* before the throne and before the four living creatures and the elders; and *no one could learn the song except the one hundred and forty-four thousand who had been purchased from the earth.* These are the ones who have not been defiled with women, for

they have kept themselves chaste. These are the ones who follow the Lamb wherever He goes. *These have been purchased from among men as first fruits* to God and to the Lamb. (Re 14:1-4)

There is a waterfall of four springs called the Banias in Galilee. They form the headwaters supplying the Galilee, or properly, the Kinneret. Kinneret is from *kinnor*, a harp. It is a voice of many waters that will run through the harp of the Kinneret and through the length of Israel all the way to the Salt Sea.

John's vision pairs the firstfruits who were purchased from among men with the sound of the chaste ones plucking and singing with their harps. Their song is "new," not one that has been gone over through repetition, a pruning action *prohibited in the year of release*. The sound of thunder and lightning accompanied the giving of the Torah "on the mountain" at Sinai through the sound of the ram's horn, in Hebrew, a *yovel*.[78]

In the years of release, the Master of the Vineyard will not "prune" the Land. It is released to grow of its own accord. It is a free growth of spiritual and natural. It responds to the spiritual Word of creation, Yeshua's complete authority. It sings a song of its own accord, inspired by Words of Spirit, not natural pruning. It rests in the previous six years of prunings (plantings and removals) worked in them.

The Torah portion Behar goes on to discuss the sixth feast of Adonai, Yom HaKippurim, as the time of blowing the Yovel. It seals up the judgments of Rosh HaShanah, which means "head of the year/ change." The traditional understanding of this Day of Blowing is that on this day, the prunings, the inclusions and removals of the new year, are declared with the blowing of the Yovel, both the silver trumpets and the ram's horn. The authority of the Judge is accepted and the judgments drawn up to be sealed on Yom HaKippurim, and then sent to be executed.

One day, the nations will be drawn to hear the song which can only be learned by those with Yeshua's authority. These firstfruits are those who have separated themselves from "women," or in plain terms spiritual idolatry. This representative number of 144,000 has been "purchased" from among men, representing the holiness of the fields and vineyards from which the firstfruits were cultivated and purchased in the previous six "years," or changes to prepare for the shmittah and Yovel changes. The moedim mark the working changes within the various kinds of firstfruits within a one-year period: barley, wheat, vegetables, fruits, clean cattle fit for sacrifice. Yom HaKippurim seals these fields of holy first fruits over to the reward of rejoicing at Sukkot.

In the Torah, what it means to be "purchased" from among men is related to firstfruits. Isaiah Five establishes that the natural vineyard is a parable of the vineyard of Israel. Adonai planted and cultivated it, yet it brought forth inferior fruit. When Judah was conquered and deported, it was for idolatry, just as it was with the Northern Kingdom of Israel. Another primary reason was that Judah did not allow the Holy Land its shmittah and Yovel years, its releases to Divine provision and growth. Natural enemies' walls, such as the Jericho's, fall when the Torah covenant is practiced. When it is not practiced, Jerusalem's walls fall.

When the authority of the Torah is not "bound in your hand" with the firstfruits at the appointed times to go up to Jerusalem, it is not practiced. The enemy, such as the Chaldeans, can breach the walls of Zion.

> You shall surely *tithe all the produce from what you sow, which comes out of the field every year.* You shall

eat in the presence of the LORD your
God, at the place where He chooses
to establish His name, the tithe of
your grain, your new wine, your oil,
and the firstborn of your herd and
your flock, so that you may learn
to fear the LORD your God always.
If the distance is so great for you that
you are not able to bring the tithe,
since the place where the LORD
your God chooses to set His name
is too far away from you when the
LORD your God blesses you, then
you shall exchange it for money,
and bind the money in your hand
and go to the place which the LORD
your God chooses. You may spend
the money for whatever your heart
desires: for oxen, or sheep, or wine, or
strong drink, or whatever your heart
desires; and there you shall eat in the
presence of the LORD your God and
rejoice, you and your household. (Dt
14:22-27)

The key in the passage above is that if the weight
of the fruit is too heavy to carry to Jerusalem, then
it may be exchanged for money, which is portable.
Once the tither arrives at the Holy City, he may
then purchase from the money whatever he needs
to celebrate. It's an economic instruction with a
spiritual application.

When a believer works and produces good fruit for
the Kingdom, it may remain upon this earth after his
death, or transplantation to the Garden to await the
resurrection. His tithes and firstfruits offered below,
however, can be exchanged for whatever his heart
desires in Jerusalem above. The faithful servant-
farmer realizes his or her own place in the vineyard
above. The faithfulness to prune over and over,
bring firstfruits and tithes with Songs of Ascent to

Jerusalem, and to rest in the appointed times, has taught the servant a song that can only be learned by the faithful.

Here is the progression pattern of holiness in redemption:

- **Tithe products are Holy**
- Firstborn of herds and flocks
- Grains, fruit of ground, fruit of the tree
- **Sell for silver money**
- Bind (compress tightly) safely into your hand because:
- Now the money is holy
- **Purchase commanded products in Jerusalem**
- The holiness passes from the money to the products
- Share and eat the products
- **All share the holiness of the original tithe that has been redeemed from among men.**

The tithe is holy, for it is a thorough representation of the holy deeds in the rest of the field, the farmer's deeds, or fruit. The rest of the field is holy because it has been redeemed by the pruned and plucked "song" of the first fruits. The farmer is in touch with holy things during the entire process, from planting to eating. In the year of release, though, it is a free, new song without ownership. All Israel, including the animals, share and eat of the holiness in the entire Land of Resurrection.

Yom HaKippurim seals the judgments of tithes and first fruits which the Israelite has "bound and compressed"[79] tightly in his hand. Likewise, Yeshua spoke of this at Hanukkah in the Temple. Hanukkah is a Jewish holiday which is celebrated as a Sukkot Sheni, or "second Sukkot" celebrated due to the Greeks' contamination of the Temple, i.e., an abomination that caused desolation. Sukkot and Hanukkah are thought to be the times when the Seven Shepherds of Sukkot and the Eight

79. tzur, the root of tribulation

116

Princes of Hanukkah, the last being Messiah, would rise up to shepherd Israel:

> My sheep hear My voice, and I know them, and they follow Me; and I give eternal life to them, and they will never perish; and *no one will snatch them out of My hand.* My Father, who has given them to Me, is greater than all; and *no one is able to snatch them out of the Father's hand.* I and the Father are one. (Jn 10:27-30)

To the Israelite farmer bringing his tithe and firstfruit money to Jerusalem is a faith that no one can snatch his "purchase" out of his hand. Likewise, those who have been purchased as firstfruits cannot be snatched out of the Father's hand. The holiness passed from the firstfruits themselves to the farmer, then to the money for which they were exchanged, then through the money to the reward of holy rejoicing in Jerusalem. Because of the farmer's faith, holiness is there from planting to reaping to journeying to rejoicing. Likewise, the holiness of the 144,000 reflects the Holy One's care in planting them, cultivating them, selecting them to represent the holiness of His fields, carrying them to Jerusalem, and welcoming them into their reward.

The 144,000 have been redeemed as first fruits to represent the holiness of the fields from which they were redeemed from the world. Their freedom song is a song of the Seventh Year of release. To the degree that the Israelites take hold of the holiness of the feasts through tribulations, they may be confident that Yeshua and the Father will forgive them, accept them, and seal them into Sukkot. They will return, every person, to his and her family in the Garden full of free fruit.

This is why we bind the commandments on our hands. It is the same as the thread tied around the first fruits of the field to mark them for holy redemption in Jerusalem. If these first fruits are faithful, then the year of release will be even more abundant! And the song? So many waters flowing through the Harp of Israel! As we bind the commandments on our hands, so Yeshua and the Father bind us into theirs, and their grip is tight!

> Wherefore the law is holy, and the commandment holy, and just, and good. (Ro 7:12)

Holy passes to holy. It is redeemed by Yeshua. Its holiness is enjoyed in New Jerusalem with the family and the Great High Priest.

Freedom and release seems to send out in the modern mindset, but in Scripture, it *gathers in* people to a place that they may not even remember if they or their ancestors departed long ago. Yovel is "freedom of movement" signaled by the yovel, the ram's horn. Before sin, Adam and Eve could freely move between spiritual and natural realms.

After sin, they fell from the wheels of fiery rivers into the natural realm, unable to return to the freedom of movement in their original home. There was a boundary between them that required a Yovel in order to return to their original homeland. In order to return to the natural Land of Israel, the Israelites had to conquer the first city by crossing the Yarden (Jordan), which means "descending." They had to go back up.

> Now Jericho was tightly shut because of the sons of Israel; no one went out and no one came in. The LORD said to Joshua, 'See, I have given Jericho *into your hand*, with its king and the valiant warriors. You shall march around the city, all the men of war circling the city once. You shall do so

for six days.

Also seven priests shall carry seven trumpets of rams' horns (*yovlim*) before the ark; then on the seventh day you shall march around the city seven times, and the priests shall blow the trumpets (*shofar*). It shall be that when they make a long blast with the ram's (*yovel*) horn, and when you hear the sound of the trumpet (*shofar*), all the people shall shout with a great shout; and the wall of the city will fall down flat, *and the people will go up every man straight ahead.*' (Jo 6:1-6)

Israel is not just a natural Land. It is a spiritual Land, and one day, the righteous will be resurrected, going up with a shout. They will be bound tightly in the Father's hand. Yeshua has been faithfully pruning the vineyard, teaching us to sing his songs that grow good fruit in the vineyard. The tighter we bind the commandments into our hands, the more it hurts, but the more secure we are in the long journey of Yeshua's holiness. If it feels as if we are being pruned repetitively, we are. Without pruning, look how much energy the vine above scatters in directions that are unfruitful. Let the Ruach HaKodesh direct our thoughts and intents, every activity that sucks production away from real fruitfulness.

The year of release to go up is just ahead. We are in the Father's hand. A new song awaits.

UPON THE ROSE OF THE HARP

Bamidbar "In the wilderness"
Numbers 1:1-4:20
Hosea 2:1-2:23
Psalm 122
Revelation 14:3-5

Mattot "Tribes"
Numbers 30:2-32:42
Jeremiah 1:1-2:3
Psalm 111
Revelation 7:1-4

Balak "Destroyer"
Numbers 22:2-25:9
Micah 5:6-6:8
Psalm 79
Revelation 2:21-23

There are 144,000 reasons to read each Torah portion. In this triple-treat of Torah portions, both the details of the portion as well as its overall story will link Revelation-readers to a foundation within it. In fact, since "The Revelation" in Judaism is the Revelation at Mount Sinai in the words of the Torah, it makes sense that John's last revelation will be rooted in its words.

For instance, John's Revelation includes specific details of the twelve tribes of Israel, both as receiving a new song and as being the very substance of the Holy City. In addition, John describes various destroyers as beasts, the antichrist, the false prophet, the dragon, and even the supernatural bugs of Abaddon. He describes the woman being carried in the wilderness to be nourished away from the presence of the serpent.

If the reader wants foundations to these destroyers, tribes, and the wilderness in the end-time Revelationary War, then he or she turns to Torah portions that highlight them: Bamidbar, Balak, and Mattot. Wilderness, Destroyer, and Tribes.

The hints in the Book of Numbers, or *Bamidbar* lend an additional seed prophecy for cross-reference. Bamidbar ("in the wilderness") emphasizes the *safeguarding* of the Mishkan in the wilderness according to one's tribe. From this emphasis on safeguarding, whose Hebrew root is *shamar*, the priests and Levites designated "watches," or terms of service in the Mishkan. This principle was later transferred to the Temple. These "watches" of the Levites made up the twenty-four watches of the Temple and the Tabernacle. Likewise, twenty-four elders keep watch in Heaven.

The number of watches (24) is the number of twelve tribes times two. Likewise, there are twenty-four elders in the Book of Revelation, such as in Revelation Four. If Moses designed the watches according to the pattern in heaven, then twenty-four watches of the priesthood and Levites makes sense. Earthly, Heavenly. The Torah portion also emphasizes that the Levites represented the twelve tribes *and* their firstborn, so perhaps the twenty-four is representative of those. Revelation emphasizes the 144,000 as the first fruits from the earth.

The twelve tribes, who had their own banners,

camped in four divisions, four directions from the Tabernacle. Each divisional banner had a graphic of the four living creatures,[80] lion, man, bull, eagle. There are also four angels at each direction who can hold back the winds, perhaps both natural and spiritual, for "wind" in Hebrew is *ruach*, also spirit.

> After this I saw four angels standing at the four corners of the earth, holding back the four winds of the earth, so that no wind would blow on the earth or on the sea or on any tree.
>
> And I saw another angel ascending from the rising of the sun, having the seal of the living God; and he cried out with a loud voice to the four angels to whom it was granted to harm the earth and the sea, saying, 'Do not harm the earth or the sea or the trees until we have sealed the bond-servants of our God on their foreheads.' And I heard the number of those who were sealed, one hundred and forty-four thousand sealed from every tribe of the sons of Israel... (Re 7:1-4).

The angels are assigned to the four corners of the earth, ready to execute judgments from Heaven when they hear a shouted command. Likewise, the tribes camped on four sides of the Tabernacle, ready to move on command when the Ark and the pillar of cloud moved.

Revelationary War History

Bamidbar's contents describe the encampments of the tribes. If the reader wants to know more about the 144,000 warriors sealed from each tribe, then he or she turns to Bamidbar, the first portion in the Book of Numbers, which *numbers the armed men of the*

80. p. 8, *Creation Gospel Workbook Five Vol 4*

tribes. Now add the Torah portion Mattot (Tribes) and Balak (Destroyer) for the context of the 12,000 armed men among the tribes in Numbers 31:

> Then the LORD spoke to Moses, saying, 'Take full vengeance for the sons of Israel on the Midianites; afterward you will be gathered to your people.' Moses spoke to the people, saying, 'Arm men from among you for the war, that they may go against Midian to execute the LORD'S vengeance on Midian. *A thousand from each tribe of all the tribes of Israel you shall send to the war.*' So there were furnished from the thousands of Israel, a thousand from each tribe, *twelve thousand armed for war.* (Nu 31:1-5)

The reader is locating context for an equal number of combatants from each tribe, a number intensified in Revelation to 144,000 (for He keeps His promises in thousands). Additionally, the context supplies another clue that makes sense when matched with texts in Revelation: the 12,000-man army of Numbers 31 is to take vengeance on Midian specifically for its sin of sending women to corrupt the Israelite men with eating things sacrificed to idols and adultery. It was the false prophet Balaam who taught Balak and the Midianite women how to do this.

> But I have a few things against you, because you have there some who hold the teaching of Balaam, who kept teaching Balak to put a stumbling block before the sons of Israel, to eat things sacrificed to idols and to commit acts of immorality. I gave her time to repent, and she does not want to repent of her immorality. Behold, I will throw her on a bed of sickness, and those who

commit adultery with her into great tribulation, unless they repent of her deeds. And I will kill her children with pestilence, and all the churches will know that I am He who searches the minds and hearts; and I will give to each one of you according to your deeds. (Re 2:21-23)

If the reader wasn't sure there was a link between the army of 12,000 in the wilderness and the army of 144,000 in Revelation, then the direct references to Balaam, Balak, eating things sacrificed to idols, and adultery nail down the issue.

The point of taking the "woman" Israel to the wilderness, or *midbar*, was to test her by nourishing her there with a type of food she'd never experienced before. Israel's test in the midbar became the substance of Yeshua's answer to the Destroyer who tempted him to make stones into bread. Yeshua said, "Man shall not live by bread alone, but by every *word* that proceeds from God's mouth."[81] The Word of Torah[82] was what sustained Moses on Mt. Sinai for two periods of forty days and forty nights. This word sustained Yeshua as well for forty days and forty nights, for he was the prophet like unto Moses and the Word made flesh.

> He humbled you and let you be hungry, and fed you with manna which you did not know, nor did your fathers know, that He might make you understand that man does not live by bread alone, but man lives by everything that proceeds out of the mouth of the LORD. (Dt 8:3)
>
> In the wilderness He fed you manna which your fathers did not know, that He might humble you and that He might test you, to do good for you in

81. Mt 4:4

82. See BEKY Book *What is the Torah?* by the author.

the end. (Dt 8:16)

The manna was the preparatory diet for entering the Promised Land, for how could one enter the Land, work it, and preserve it as Adam was intended to do without developing a taste for the Word and its nourishment from above?

> The manna ceased on the day after they had eaten some of the produce of the land, so that the sons of Israel no longer had manna, but they ate some of the yield of the land of Canaan during that year.
> (Jo 5:12)

The wilderness was when the Israelites walked in clouds of glory. Few realized why the Egyptian food and water was taken away. Egypt was a dry reed that could not support them in their destination. What is often overlooked about the wilderness experience is that it was full of the instruction of the Holy Spirit, the Ruach HaKodesh. Just as Yeshua promised his disciples that the Ruach HaKodesh would instruct them what to say,[83] so the Ruach instructed the Israelites in the Word through the manna and water from Heaven, Yeshua:

> You gave Your good Spirit to instruct them, Your manna You did not withhold from their mouth, and You gave them water for their thirst. (Ne 9:20)

Good spirit = manna, water

Sadly, the instruction mostly did not fall on good soil in the first wilderness generation. Their children, though, followed Joshua into the Promised Land.

83. Jn 14:26

What a great reminder to come into the Kingdom like a little child!

The Red One

Another context for a 12,000-man army is the army of Edom, which was defeated by David and Joab:

> For the choir director; according to Shushan Eduth. A Mikhtam of David, to teach; when he struggled with Aram-naharaim and with Aram-zobah, and Joab returned, and smote twelve thousand of Edom in the Valley of Salt. (Ps 60:1)

Edom is known in Jewish literature as "The Red One" who will be defeated by Messiah. Perhaps it is no coincidence that the fifth assembly of Revelation is Sardis, which means "Red Ones." This lends a more ominous tone to the Sardis warning, which followed the warning to Thyatira. Thyratira was an assembly that was leading the righteous astray because it encouraged them to eat things offered to idols through the agency of the "Jezebel woman." This is the exact sin of Midian. They led the Israelite men astray through adultery and idolatry, starting with things offered to Baal-Peor. Psalm 60 continues:

> O God, You have rejected us. You have broken us; You have been angry; O, restore us. You have made the land quake, You have split it open; heal its breaches, for it totters. You have made Your people experience hardship; You have given us wine to drink that makes us stagger. You have given a banner to those who fear You, that it may be displayed because of the truth. Selah. That Your beloved may be delivered, save with Your right hand, and answer us!

God has spoken in His holiness: 'I will exult, I will portion out Shechem and measure out the valley of Succoth. Gilead is Mine, and Manasseh is Mine; Ephraim also is the helmet of My head; Judah is My scepter. Moab is My washbowl; *over Edom I shall throw My shoe*; shout loud, O Philistia, because of Me! Who will bring me into the besieged city? Who will lead me to Edom? Have not You Yourself, O God, rejected us? *And will You not go forth with our armies, O God?* O give us help against the adversary, for deliverance by man is in vain. Through God we shall do valiantly, and it is He who will tread down our adversaries.'

Psalm 60 began with a reference to the theme of 12,000, which is the defeat of Edom in the Valley of Salt. Edom is "The Red One," representing the soul, the *nefesh*, the bundle of appetites, emotions, and desires that war against the spirit of a man. It is what man has in common with a beast.

The Artscroll commentary on Psalm 60 helps the reader to make the thematic connections among the encampment of the tribes, the 12,000 who defeated the Midianites to execute Adonai's revenge, and the selection of 12,000 from each tribe to total the representative number of all Israel, 144,000:

> This psalm presents David's inspired vision of a universal order of nations united in complete harmony. This was his dream. The concept of universal peace is a manifestation of monotheism, the belief in one Almighty God. Pagan mythology depicts a chaotic heaven torn asunder by jealous, warring 'gods' who are no

more than an exaggerated reflection of their human creators. *Struggle, conflict, and polarization are basic elements of the idolator's worldview.*

The Jew, who believes in one Creator, believes that all of the diverse elements of this universe are basically united to serve the purposes of the one God, Who gives order to the world. Israel is at the center of this world order, and the supreme tribunal of this nations, the Great Sanhedrin, convenes in the Temple, which is the spiritual center of the earth. Each of the seventy members of this august body is symbolic of one of the world's seventy nations, and the seventy-first member, the chief justice, represents Israel, the nation which controls the order of all other peoples. (Ramban to Numbers 11:16, quoted in *The Tehillim*, p. 745).

This psalm records a rare time when David went on the offensive instead of defensive in the war against Edom, who represented the nations. The two entities he attacked had already broken pacts with him: Aram Naharaim and Aram Tzovah. According to the commentators, "It was necessary to take the offensive to subjugate the nations in order to prepare for universal peace, represented by his son Solomon's reign." It was in this Messianic archetypal war that David and Joab struck down 12,000 Red Ones. The psalm was to be played upon a Shushan Edut, or a "rose of testimony," possibly a harp shaped like a rose.[84]

Edut holds the Hebrew root *ed*, which forms so many vital words: testimony (*edut*), eternity (*ad*) jewelry (*adi*), witness (*edah*), assembly (*adat*), feast (*moed*). The Rose must have been a very beautiful instrument.

84. ibid, p. 746

The English rendering of "when he made war" (*b'hatzoto*) against Aram Naharaim and Aram Tzovah" has a double entendre, a poetic turn of phrase in Hebrew: "B'hatzoto et Aram Naharaim veh-et Aram Tzovah..." The roots of war and Tzovah are the same in Hebrew, and as suggested by the Jewish sage Ibn Ezra, it means "destroy." The wordplay is found in the statement that David destroyed the [high place, Aram] destroyer and set it on fire.[85] Again, this is a Messianic turn of phrase. Balak also means "Destroyer."

David also destroyed Aram Naharaim, the high place of the Rivers. This river is understood to be the Euphrates, which is also called the Great River. In Hebrew, it is the Perat River of Eden. The Midrash *Shocher Tov* suggests that David actually split this river so that it would not block his army when he attacked Aram.[86] Revelation alludes to this "drying up" of the Euphrates for the Kings of the East to draw them into a final war of their destruction.[87]

Verses three and four of Psalm 60 mention two of the three components that comprise Israel: Land, Covenant, and People. The Covenant is understood from its being played upon the Shushan Edut, the beautiful rose of testimony. David records also the quaking of the land itself along with the breaking of the people in His wrath. He begs mercy, return, and healing of the fragments. Such earthquakes are also recorded in Revelation.[88]

David mentions that Israel was forced to drink "benumbing wine." The commentators parse the Hebrew and conclude that this wine "arouses the world to undo the burden of Torah." In Revelation, a cup of wrath is also forced upon the world.[89] The world will likewise be shattered. "The world is only considered to be united when Israel is recognized by all nations as the center of world affairs, for it says, 'Jacob is the bond (which keeps together all the

85. p. 747

86. p. 748

87. Re 16:12

88. Re 6:12; 8:5; 11:13; 11:19; 16:18

89. Re 14:10; 16:19

nations) of His estate.'"[90]

Verse eight mentions dividing portions, which "refers to enemy property which would be apportioned to the Jewish exiles returning from the Diaspora,"[91] and in another reference to the nations, David calls it "the Valley of Sukkot" that will be measured out. Sukkot is the Feast of the Nations. It is also called Shechem, which is where Jacob camped when he re-entered the Land of Israel, and he built sukkot for his cattle. In Psalm 60:9, "Judah is my lawgiver," suggesting that Judah will organize this return and assigning of the inheritance, just as in Bamidbar it is Judah who sets out first once the trumpets blow. This context of blowing trumpets also appears in Revelation.[92]

In Revelation, the 144,000, which is 12,000 from each tribe, have defining characteristics:

> And they sang a new song before the throne and before the four living creatures and the elders; and no one could learn the song except the one hundred and forty-four thousand who had been purchased from the earth. *These are the ones who have not been defiled with women, for they have kept themselves chaste.* These are the ones who follow the Lamb wherever He goes. *These have been purchased from among men as first fruits* to God and to the Lamb. And no lie was found in their mouth; they are blameless. (Re 14:3-5)

As with the numbering of the tribes for representation by the Levites and the redemption, or purchasing of the first born, so the 144,000 is a representative number chosen as a first fruits representative of the vast numbers who have not been defiled by Midianite women with food sacrificed to idols,

90. Dt 32:9, ibid

91. Rashi, p. 753

92. Re 8:2,6

adultery, or idolatry. They are also true witnesses, having "no lie," which recalls the Rose of Testimony, a beautiful harp instrument to sing truth:

> Then I looked, and behold, the Lamb was standing on Mount Zion, and with Him one hundred and forty-four thousand, having His name and the name of His Father written on their foreheads. And I heard a voice from heaven, *like the sound of many waters* and like the sound of loud thunder, and the voice which I heard *was like the sound of harpists playing on their harps.* (Re 14:1-2)

The "many waters" are found in Balak when Balaam involuntarily blesses of the twelve tribes:

> How fair are your tents, O Jacob,
> Your dwellings, O Israel!
> Like valleys that stretch out,
> Like gardens beside the river,
> Like aloes planted by the LORD,
> Like cedars beside the waters.
> Water will flow from his buckets,
> And *his seed will be by many waters*,
> And his king shall be higher than Agag,
> And his kingdom shall be exalted. (Ex 24:5-7)

In the context of Mattot, or "Tribes," Moses tells the people to select armed men. This command to the tribes follows the annulment of vows. If one does not perform a vow, then he or she is a liar unless legally nullifying words follow.[93] That passage is preceded by a summary of the feasts, which are also designated in Revelation under the messages to the seven assemblies.[94] All the themes are connected in Revelation.

93. Nu 30:7

Revelation describes the 144,000 as men having the Name of the Father written on their foreheads. The armed men were to be men of righteousness, and therefore they would be men who obeyed the commandment to "Hear O Israel..." This is performed when Jewish males put *tefillin* on the arm and forehead for prayer each day. The parchments within the boxes of those tefillin contain the Sacred Name.[95]

The vengeance on Midian was for the spiritual and natural adultery (idolatry) committed by the men of Israel with the Midianites under Balaam's teaching. A righteous man, Pinchas, is dispatched to finish the job he began with spearing Cozbi and Zimri in the act of idolatrous adultery. Now this makes sense:

> Now the name of the slain man of Israel who was slain with the Midianite woman, was Zimri the son of Salu, a leader of a father's household among the Simeonites. The name of the Midianite woman who was slain was Cozbi the daughter of Zur, who was head of the people of a father's household in Midian. (Nu 25:14-15)

Zimri was the Israelite man who cohabited with the adulterous Midianite woman. Zimri means "melody, song." In Revelation, the 144,000 turn the tables with truth, and they sing a different tune with the Rose of Testimony!

Let's return to Revelation for additional clues to the Torah portion prophecies:

a. The list of tribes sealed in Revelation is missing the tribe of Dan.

b. In the Torah portion Balak, the 78,000 elders had to kill two adulterers apiece.[96]

c. 156,000 killed for adultery in Balak.

94. See *Creation Gospel Workbook One*'s section on "The Seven Assemblies of Revelation" for a complete explanation of how the seven assemblies represent Passover, Unleavened Bread, First fruits of the Barley, First fruits of the Wheat, Trumpets, Atonements, and Tabernacles.

95. See *Creation Gospel Workbook Two* for a complete discussion of the tefillin and the beast's number of 666.

d. -12,000 missing from tribe of Dan in Revelation 7:4-8

144,000

Pinchas' action against Zimri and Cozbi stopped the spreading plague, or pestilence:

> But I have a few things against you, because you have there some who hold the teaching of **Balaam, who kept teaching Balak** to put a stumbling block before the sons of Israel, to eat things sacrificed to idols and to commit acts of immorality. I gave her time to repent, and she does not want to repent of her immorality. Behold, **I will throw her on a bed** of sickness, and **those who commit adultery with her** into great tribulation, unless they repent of her deeds. And I will **kill her children with pestilence**, and all the churches will know that I am He who searches the minds and hearts; and I will give to each one of you according to your deeds. (Re 2:21-23)

John gives more context clues by linking the teaching of Balaam with spiritual adultery, which Adonai equates with the works of Jezebel. The pestilence on the children is the proof of an adulterous woman who has violated her vows. Vows are the context of Mattot, both men AND women.

If Elijah is one of the two witnesses (with Moses) in Revelation, now we have more context for the wilderness (Bamidbar prophecy):

96. According to Rashi's commentary on the portion.

1. an oath or vow

2. spiritual adultery or those who have not

134

defiled themselves with women

3. the prophet Elijah, who, according to tradition, will designate who is a member of which tribe upon their return, possibly both to be assigned an inheritance in the Land and as an army to take vengeance on Midian/Jezebel/Balaam spiritual adulterers and idolators

4. the wilderness (*midbar*) as a place of escape

The tour through the Bible continues! Now Elijah joins the "in the wilderness" conversation:

> Now Ahab told Jezebel all that Elijah had done, and how he had killed all the prophets with the sword. Then Jezebel sent a messenger to Elijah, saying, 'So may the gods do to me and even more, if I do not make your life as the life of one of them by tomorrow about this time.' And he was afraid and arose and ran for his life and came to Beersheba, which belongs to Judah, and left his servant there. But he himself went a day's journey into the wilderness, and came and sat down under a juniper tree... (1 Ki 19:1-4)

Queen Jezebel is angry that the false prophets have been killed, so she takes a vow, and King Ahab does not annul it, which is the procedure outlined in Mattot. Jezebel cannot perform the vow, and as a result, she dies. The gods she believed in were not so kind as to forgive a broken vow.

Again there is a Revelation link, the iconic false prophet, such as Balaam. Elijah, the true prophet, goes to the wilderness expecting to die, yet an angel prepares a place for him and nourishes him.

> And she gave birth to a son, a male child, who is to rule all the nations with a rod of iron; and her child was caught up to God and to His throne. Then the woman fled into the wilderness where she had a place prepared by God, so that there she would be nourished for one thousand two hundred and sixty days. (Re 12:5-6)

Here is the Jewish expectation of a ruler from Israel who will rule the nations. The birth of the child was vindication of the "woman's" faithfulness and fidelity to her vows to her Husband, for the innocent woman who was tested in a vow brought forth healthy children, not the children to be killed by pestilence. In the wilderness, Elijah is told that there are 7,000 more like him who had not bent the knee to Baal.[97]

> But the two wings of the great eagle were given to the woman, so that she could fly into the wilderness to her place, where she was nourished for a time and times and half a time, from the presence of the serpent. (Re 12:14)

Elijah represents righteous Israel being taken to the wilderness for protection and testing, just as Adonai took them before in Deuteronomy 34:11 and Jeremiah 2:2. Like Jezebel, there is an adulterous woman in Revelation who is in league with a false prophet for a beast and a serpent:

> And he carried me away in the Spirit into a wilderness; and I saw a woman sitting on a scarlet beast, full of blasphemous names... (Re 17:3)

Edom is The Red One, the Scarlet Beast, a king to be defeated by David's offspring who will rule the nations and prepare an era of peace.

97. 1 Ki 19:18

136

So the Scriptures present contrast and choice. Is a believer aligned with apostate Israel whoring in the desert with idolatrous behaviors, or is she righteous Israel hiding from evil, sealed in the Torah, and awaiting the trumpet call to war against the King of Edom (the Red One, the Beast), the False Prophet, and the Dragon? Both Israels go to the wilderness, but one will bear the fruit of righteousness, and the other will die with her idolatrous fruit.

As we camp in the wilderness, so shall our journey be to Sukkot and the Kingdom.

10

THE GREAT HALLEL

The Great Hallel
Psalm 113-118

What is the one Hebrew word that almost everyone universally knows?

Hallelujah!

Hallelu means "we praise," and jah is "Yah," the shortened form of the Sacred Name. We praise Yah! Praise is often transmitted in song. Although all human beings can appreciate music and sing, and the living creatures have their own song of praise, musicians are especially blessed with song.

With such a great gift from Heaven's treasury of shining jewels, musicians and singers bear a huge responsibility. Most of the music written in the world today glorifies mankind. Much of it glorifies man's sinfulness, so it is off-key no matter how memorable it may be. Such songs are a departure from the definition and purpose of a *shir*, a song. The *definition* of a shir is:

1.   The performance of God's will

2. Recognition that He and He alone is the Master of the heavenly and earthly regions, and that He and He alone is to be feared, loved, and served above all others.

The *purpose* is defined with zamar, the root of *zamir*, a different form of song, or music itself:

Sow your field ≈ prune your vineyard

Zamar[98] is to trim something, often something to be burned, cut off, or removed. It also means to plant in a vineyard as one sows a field. The field is the world.[99] The seed is the Word[100] sown into the field. Israel is the vineyard.[101] As each musician or singer composes a song or sings one, important choices are made. It is a human responsibility as a created being to cut off, burn, and trim the words of songs even as the notes, cadence, and tempo are trimmed and shaped into another beautiful plant in the vineyard.

The vineyard is holy. The field belongs to the Master of Creation. What if a musician sows lyrics into the world that defile it and will later be burned up as thorns and tares sown among the good crops? Instead of submitting these lyrics to a producer or copyright office, imagine if the artist had to first submit the lyrics to the Heavenly Court for validation before sowing the words into the soul of the world?

This doesn't mean that songs can't reflect upon the beauty of being human. Such beauty in love, passion, determination, devotion, courage, patriotism, etc., can glorify the One who created us to reflect His image and qualities. He created us to have meaningful relationships with other human beings, and it is our responsibility to make sure those relationships are more than just good, but very good. It is not good to be alone. Music can bind people together for goodness, which does glorify the Creator.

98. Zamar spelled backward in Hebrew spells *remez*, which means to imply something. A song should always imply or hint to the Creator of the universe.

99. Mt 13:38

100. Lk 8:11

101. Is 5:1-10

140

It is when those words glorify the emotion of love, for instance, over love within holy boundaries, that the composer defies the Creator. A songwriter or singer is the keeper of a vineyard. He or she is a sower of seed in the field of the world. This is why it is so important for a musician to do more than casually read the Word. He must be able to prune away seed-words in his soul that are purely soul-expressions that did not come from the Holy Spirit, nor do they conform to "It is written..." It is as simple as turning one's creative work away from "I think..., I feel..., I want..." to "*It is written*, therefore, I think..., I feel..., I want..."

Hallelujah.

Any musician or singer who serves the Most High has a responsibility to know the "songs in the night." These songs are the guardrails, yet also the open doors for the musician to regard as he or she composes and sings. If the song reflects the principles taught in the "songs in the night," then it is on a very solid foundation. The songs in the night are the Great Hallel, Psalms 113-118. The Great Hallel is sung at the conclusion of every Passover meal.

Even if spoken in unison without singing it, the words build into a singsong, those gathered speak with great unity, and the passion of it builds tempo until the responsive lines of Psalm 118, "His mercy endures forever!" When the final verse is proclaimed, "Give thanks to the LORD, for He is good; for His mercy is everlasting," it is as if Heaven itself descends into the room. There is no congregational song that produces the same unity of words and purpose that Yeshua prayed for his disciples to have. It is the Great Hallel that is thought to be the "songs in the night" to which Isaiah refers:

> *You will have songs as in the night when you keep the festival*, and gladness of heart as when one

marches to the sound of the flute,
to go to the mountain of the LORD,
to the Rock of Israel. And the LORD
will cause His voice of authority to
be heard, and the descending of
His arm to be seen in fierce anger,
and in the flame of a consuming
fire in cloudburst, downpour, and
hailstones. (Is 30:29-30)

At each Passover, the family recites the Hallel. This
describes the songs of praise, not just at the Sea
of Reeds on the march to the Mountain, but the
night Israel celebrated the Passover by singing the
Hallel. Songs of praise should celebrate salvation,
redemption, hope, faith, holiness, and yes, even
judgment. The English word for music and musician
comes from Muse, attributing the gift to ancient Greek
goddesses presiding over the arts and sciences. This
does not mean that musicians are idol-worshipers! It
does, however, point to the influence that idols have
in our language.

Glorifying human creativity over the Creator instead
of attributing to and dedicating it to the Creator is
modern idolatry. No Muse-goddess created human
beings or their inspiration to compose or perform
music. Musicians have a special opportunity to repair
humankind's contribution to the songs of Creation.
They can turn listeners' thoughts away from idols
of human glory and toward thoughts of Heavenly
glory. They prune the vineyard of Israel and sow the
field of the world! Often it is how the composer trims
the notes of a catchy sing-along that lures listeners
into singing lyrics with which their spirits most certainly
do not agree!

The Hallel includes a passage from Psalm 115:4-
8, which equates idols with the dead. Huldah's
prophecy assured King Josiah that Judah's
102. 2 Ch 34:22- punishment for idolatry would not occur before
28 his death.[102] Death was coming, but the king)s

142

sincere repentance provided a stay of execution for the dead, those who worshiped idols and became "like them," dead. In Messiah Yeshua, believers are no longer dead, but practicing lives of resurrection even before the human body is resurrected. The Great Hallel is a song of salvation, and the Jewish sages point out:

> Israel will sing the song of praise upon the Messianic Redemption, a song that will resemble the song they sang on the night of the Passover in Egypt, the Song of Hallel. (Midrash Rabbah to Shir HaShirim, 2§1)

Since the Great Hallel's ultimate message is resurrection from the dead, then any song ever written or sung must have life in order to endure forever. If a song's lyrics proclaim disobedience to the Holy One, it will die and pass out of the consciousness of the resurrected dead. The Heavenly Court will not permit such words to pass into eternity. Instead, they will fall into the realm of death, their true "hometown." The righteous will live in the obedience of praise for eternity, untainted by dead words and works. Praise in song is so important to coming before the Holy One that it is considered a holy sacrifice![103]

> The Great Hallel is sung at three major feasts of Israel: Passover, Pentecost, and Tabernacles. It is also seen as the "Rose of Sharon" song:
>
> I am the Rose of Sharon, the Lily of the Valley. (So 2:1)

The Hebrew Scriptures are full of wordplay, enhancing the meaning of many words and passages. "The Rose of Sharon" is one of those phrases. *Sharon* is a place in Israel, but when a Hebrew letter *nun* ("n" sound) is added to the end of a word, it creates a noun construct denoting finality or permanence. In

103. He 13:15

such a case, the pronunciation of the word is slightly altered.

Sharon can then be read as a play-on the word shir. Shir is a song, and Sharon is the *permanent and final* song. It is the song of resurrection to the original Creation perfection. The Rose of Sharon, then describes the state of the permanent Song, or Sharon. Roses have a slow, but beautiful transformation from a small, tight bud to full flower. Every day the rose looks different, and it goes from a bud that sheds most of the rain and dew that falls on it to an open flower that captures the dew and raindrops.

The Hallel as "Ha-sharon" is the rose that is still unopened to receive the dew of Heaven. The message of the Great Hallel is still muted among the nations of the earth. This song is a way of saying,

> Tomorrow when the Holy One redeems me from the shadow of these foreign kingdoms, I will be saturated with showers and dew and blossom forth like a rose, and utter before Him a new song of praise: 'Sing to the LORD a new song, for He has done wonders; His own right hand and holy arm have helped Him.' (Midrash Rabbah to Shir HaShirim 2§1 & Ps 98:1)

All over the world, musicians and singers have a priceless opportunity to sow in the field of the nations and prune the vineyard of Israel. Sometimes writers sow words as sacrifices of praise, and sometimes they sacrifice by not writing words. If an idea praises something in the realm of death and disobedience, the pruning away of that idea is a sacrifice as well. A petal should open only for the dew and rain of the truth in the Word.

The multiple instructions in the Torah concerning the first fruits and tithes link the reader to the three feasts of Israel when the produce was brought to the Temple and Jerusalem. The pilgrims walked in groups to Jerusalem singing the Songs of Ascents, hinting to the resurrection from the dead when the righteous will rise. They brought sacrifices accompanied by praise. Imagine how their songs resounded throughout the Land of Israel, growing in enthusiasm as they neared the Holy City. Imagine their anticipation as an opening flower. A song of life endures forever.

By composing and singing faithful songs, the Rose of Sharon will open a little more every day until Messiah returns. Israel will begin to capture the teaching of the Word like morning dew on its open, perfect petals:

> May my teaching drip as the rain,
> My speech trickle as the dew,
> As droplets on the fresh grass,
> And as the showers on the vegetation.
> (Dt 32:2)

Music can be part of resurrection life by being "songs in the night." Music can function in its intended role, to awaken Israel in the night so that she can be prepared for the dawn of resurrection. The Great Hallel, the "festival" song of resurrection, builds to the crescendo of Psalm 118. See how the awakening from the night comes, and how Israel responds to each resurrection "call" in 118, acknowledging her resurrection, bringing forth her hidden treasures. Imagine the family sitting around the Passover table in the night, singing the Great Hallel in Egypt. They obeyed the Word, and their petals capture the dew in the night. Their resurrection from death will come with the dawn.

> Your dead will live;
> Their corpses will rise.
> You who lie in the dust, awake and shout for joy,

For your dew is as the dew of the dawn,
And the earth will give birth to the departed spirits. (Is 26:19)

His mercy endures forever. Hallelujah!

REFERENCES

Alewine, H. (2019). *50,000 Degrees and Cloudy: A Better Resurrection*. London, KY: BEKY Books.

Feuer, A. (2002). *The Tehillim*. Vol I: Psalms 1-72. New York: Mesorah Publications, Ltd.

Kahn, A. (2011). *Echoes of Eden: Sefer Bereishit*. Springfield, NJ: Gefen Books.

_____ (2012). *Echoes of Eden: Sefer Shemot*. Springfield, NJ: Gefen Books.

Weissman, M. (1980). *The Midrash Says*. New York: Benei Yakov Publications.

Scherman, N. (Trans.) (2004). *Perek Shirah*. New York: Mesorah Publication, Ltd.

Scherman, N. & Zlotowitz, M., Eds. (2020). *The Midrash: Chamesh Megillot*. Shir HaShirim Vol I: Ch 1-3. Milstein Ed. New York: Mesorah Publications, Ltd.

Scherman, N. & Zlotowitz, M., Eds. (1997). *The Torah: With Rashi's commentary translated, annotated, and elucidated*. Sapirstein Ed. New York: Mesorah Publications, Ltd.

APPENDIX A

Names and Meanings of the Weekly Parshiot

Torah Portion (*Parasha*) Name	Torah Reading	Haftorah	Psalm
	GENESIS		
Bereshit, בְּרֵאשִׁית In the beginning	Ge 1:1-6:8	Is 42:5-43:11	139
Noach, נֹחַ Rest	Ge 6:9-11:3	Is 54:1-55:5	29
Lech-Lecha, לֶךְ-לְךָ Go for yourself!	Ge 12:1-17:27	Is 40:27-41:16	110
Vayeira, וַיֵּרָא And He appeared	Ge 18:1-22:24	2 Ki 4:1-37	11
Chayei Sarah, חַיֵּי שָׂרָה Life of Sarah	Ge 23:1-25:18	1 Ki 1:1-31	45
Toledot, תּוֹלְדֹת Generations	Ge 25:19-28:9	Mal 1:1-2:7	36
Vayetze, וַיֵּצֵא And went out	Ge 28:10-32:3	Hos 12:13-14:10	3
Vayishlach, וַיִּשְׁלַח And sent	Ge 32:4-36:43	Hos 11:7-12:12 Ob 1:1-21	140
Vayeshev, וַיֵּשֶׁב And settled	Ge 37:1-40:23	Amos 2:6-3:8	112
Miketz, מִקֵּץ At the end	Ge 41:1-44:17	1 Ki 3:15-4:1	40
Vayigash, וַיִּגַּשׁ And drew near	Ge 44:18-47:27	Ezek 37:15-37:28	48
Vayechi, וַיְחִי And lived	Ge 47:28-50:26	1 Ki 2:1-12	41

EXODUS			
Shemot, שְׁמוֹת Names	Ex 1:1-6:1	Is 27:6-28:13; 29:22-23	99
Va'eira, וָאֵרָא And I appeared	Ex 6:2-9:35	Ezek 28:25- 29:21	46
Bo, בֹּא Enter!	Ex 10:1-13:16	Je 46:13-46:28	77
Beshalach, בְּשַׁלַּח When he sent out	Ex 13:17-17:16	Judges 4:4-5:31	66
Yitro, יִתְרוֹ Jethro	Ex 18:1-20:23	Is 6:1-7:6; 9:5-6	19
Mishpatim, מִשְׁפָּטִים Statutes	Ex 21:1-24:18	Je 34:8-34:22; 33:25-26	72
Terumah, תְּרוּמָה Offering	Ex 25:1-27:19	1 Ki 5:26-6:13	26
Tetzaveh, תְּצַוֶּה You shall command	Ex 27:20-30:10	Ezek 43:10- 43:27	65
Ki Tisa, כִּי תִשָּׂא When you elevate	Ex 30:11-34:35	1 Ki 18:1-18:39	75
Vayakhel, וַיַּקְהֵל And he assembled	Ex 35:1-38:20	1 Ki 7:40-50	61
Pekudei, פְקוּדֵי Accountings of	Ex 38:21-40:38	1 Ki 7:51-8:21	45

LEVITICUS			
Vayikra, וַיִּקְרָא And called	Le 1:1-5:26	Is 43:21-44:23	50
Tzav, צַו Command!	Le 6:1-8:36	Je 7:21-8:3; 9:22-23	107
Shemini, שְׁמִינִי Eighth	Le 9:1-11:47	2 Sa 6:1-7:17	128
Tazria, תַזְרִיעַ She sows seed	Le 12:1-13:59	2 Ki 4:42-5:19	106
Metzora, מְצֹרָע Infected one	Le 14:1-15:33	2 Ki 7:3-20	120
Acharei Mot, אַחֲרֵי מוֹת After the death	Le 16:1-18:30	Ezek 22:1-22:19	26
Kedoshim, קְדֹשִׁים Holies	Le 19:1-20:27	Amos 9:7-9:15	15
Emor, אֱמֹר Say!	Le 21:1-24:23	Ezek 44:15- 44:31	42
Behar, בְּהַר On the mountain	Le 25:1-26:2	Je 32:6-32:27	112
Bechukotai, בְּחֻקֹּתַי In My statutes	Le 26:3-27:34	Je 16:19-17:14	105

NUMBERS			
Bamidbar, בְּמִדְבַּר **In the wilderness**	Nu 1:1-4:20	Hosea 2:1-2:23	122
Naso, נָשֹׂא **Lift up!**	Nu 4:21-7:89	Judges 13:2-13:25	67
Behaalotecha, בְּהַעֲלֹתְךָ **In your making go up**	Nu 8:1-12:16	Zech 2:14-4:7	68
Shlach, שְׁלַח-לְךָ **Send for yourself**	Nu 13:1-15:41	Josh 2:1-2:24	64
Korach, קֹרַח **Korach (bald)**	Nu 16:1-18:32	1 Sa 11:14-12:22	5
Chukat, חֻקַּת **Ordinance of**	Nu 19:1-22:1	Judges 11:1-33	95
Balak, בָּלָק **Destroyer**	Nu 22:2-25:9	Micah 5:6-6:8	79
Pinchas, פִּינְחָס **Phinehas**	Nu 25:10-30:1	1 Ki 18:46-19:21	50
Mattot, מַטּוֹת **Tribes**	Nu 30:2-32:42	Je 1:1-2:3	111
Masei, מַסְעֵי **Journeys of**	Nu 33:1-36:13	Je 2:4-28; 3:4	49

DEUTERONOMY			
Devarim, דְּבָרִים Words	Dt 1:1-3:22	Is 1:1-27	137
Va'etchanan, וָאֶתְחַנַּן And pleaded	Dt 3:23-7:11	Is 40:1-26	90
Eikev, עֵקֶב As a result	Dt 7:12-11:25	Is 49:14-51:3	75
Re'eh, רְאֵה See!	Dt 11:26-16:17	Is 54:11-55:5	97
Shoftim, שֹׁפְטִים Judges	Dt 16:18-21:9	Is 51:12-52:12	17
Ki Teitzei, כִּי-תֵצֵא When you go out	Dt 21:10-25:19	Is 54:1-10	32
Ki Tavo, כִּי-תָבוֹא When you enter in	Dt 26:1-29:8	Is 60:1-22	51
Nitzavim, נִצָּבִים You are standing	Dt 29:9-30:20	Is 61:10-63:9	81
Vayelech, וַיֵּלֶךְ And went	Dt 31:1-31:30	Is 55:6-56:8	65
Haazinu, הַאֲזִינוּ Give ear!	Dt 32:1-32:52	2 Sa 22:1-51	71
V'Zot HaBerachah וְזֹאת הַבְּרָכָה And this the blessing	Dt 33:1-34:12	Joshua 1:1-18	12

APPENDIX B

Example of How the Parasha Names Summarize a Book of Torah

The Story in Portions
Book One: Genesis
Bereishit: בְּרֵאשִׁית

Bereishit **"In the Beginning"** Elohim placed Adam and Eve in the Garden. They sinned, and were driven from the Garden. Violence and robbery covered the earth, but through flood in the time of *Noach*, the earth could **"rest."** The world once again turned to wickedness through idolatry, so Avram was told to *Lekh Lekha* and **"go for yourself"** to the Promised Land. And the Lord **"appeared"** *Vayera* to Abraham at his tent door and promised him a son from Sarah.

Abraham honored **"the life of Sarah,"** *Chayei Sarah*, by burying her in Hebron and finding a righteous wife for Isaac. The **"generations of"** *Toldot* Isaac are his father Avraham and his two very different sons, Esau and Jacob. In fear of Esau, Jacob *Vayetzei* **"went out"** to Haran to search for a righteous bride, and he married Rachel and Leah.

Jacob wrestled in his return to Canaan, and in fear of Esau, he *Vayishlach* **"sent"** messengers with gifts to Esau, and the meeting went well, yet his family experienced many troubles. When Jacob **"settled"** *Vayeshev* in Canaan, his sons became bitter against Joseph and sold him into slavery. *Miketz* **"at the end"** of Joseph's captivity, he interpreted Pharaoh's dream and was promoted to second in Egypt.

When Judah *Vayigash* **"drew near"** Joseph to offer himself in the place of Benjamin, Joseph revealed himself to his brothers and settled them in Goshen.

Jacob and his family *Vayechi* **"lived"** in Egypt where he blessed them, and where eventually Jacob and Joseph died.

STUDY QUESTIONS

1. Is there any evidence of reading the Word on a specific schedule in the Bible? Where?

2. What connection does every human being have to the city of Jerusalem and the Temple Mount? What is the name of "the place"?

3. What is the play-on the word in the Hebrew word for frog? What is the frog's song?

4. What is the definition of a song? Which of the "Ten Songs" has yet to be sung?

5. Why would Yeshua's beginning his ministry in the Galilee be significant? To which song is it related?

6. What is the service that *accompanies* the service of assembling, servicing, dismantling, and carrying the Tent of Meeting?

7. Yeshua the Nazarene in Aramaic, Yeshua HaNotzri, may also be understood as _____.

8. The cantillation mark called the _____
denotes someone who is lingering or having second thoughts. The lesson is that when believers pray or obey, they should not be _____ in their requests or actions.

9. How is a singer or composer similar to the keeper of a vineyard?

10. The "Songs in the night" are also known as the _____
_____.

ABOUT THE AUTHOR

Dr. Hollisa Alewine has her B.S. and M.Ed. from Texas A&M and a Doctorate from Oxford Graduate School; she is the author of Standing with Israel: A House of Prayer for All Nations, The Creation Gospel Bible study series, and a programmer on Hebraic Roots Network. Dr. Alewine is a student and teacher of the Word of God.

OTHER BOOKS
IN THIS SERIES

What is the Torah?
Introduction to Jewish Sources
Colossal Controversies
Messianic Shabbat Service
The Biblical New Moon
Divorce & Remarriage in the Bible
Truth, Tradition, or Tare
Peter's Vision
The Sabbath
Growing in Holiness
The Seven Shepherds
First Century Word
Pharisee: Friend or Foe?
The Three Days and Nights of Messiah
50,000 Degrees and Cloudy
Esther's Mysteries

www.bekybooks.com

Made in the USA
Las Vegas, NV
09 May 2022